Lyman Haynes Low

Catalogue Of The Collection Of Ancient Greek And Roman Coins

Lyman Haynes Low

Catalogue Of The Collection Of Ancient Greek And Roman Coins

ISBN/EAN: 9783741126710

Manufactured in Europe, USA, Canada, Australia, Japa

Cover: Foto ©Thomas Meinert / pixelio.de

Manufactured and distributed by brebook publishing software
(www.brebook.com)

Lyman Haynes Low

Catalogue Of The Collection Of Ancient Greek And Roman Coins

AUCTION SALE

OF

COINS and MEDALS

COLLECTIONS OF

NATHAN BELCHER

AND

THOMAS H. SHEPPARD,

With Several Consignments.

On Thursday and Friday, October 15 and 16, 1896.

AT No. 19 EAST 14th STREET,

NEW YORK CITY.

CATALOGUE

OF THE COLLECTION OF

ANCIENT GREEK AND ROMAN COINS,

INCLUDING MANY SPECIMENS, OF THE RARER SORT, OF EMPERORS AND
EMPRESSES, NOT OFTEN REPRESENTED IN COLLECTIONS.

TOGETHER WITH

MODERN COINS, MEDALS AND TOKENS,

Among which are some of the rarest HARD TIMES TOKENS AND STORE CARDS,

formed by the late

NATHAN BELCHER,

Of NEW LONDON, CONN.

ALSO THE COLLECTION BELONGING TO

THOMAS H. SHEPPARD,

Of PITTSBURGH, PENN.

CONSISTING OF ANCIENT, MODERN EUROPEAN,

UNITED STATES AND SOUTH AMERICAN COINS AND MEDALS,

SUPPLEMENTED TO THESE ARE OTHER VARIOUS CONSIGNMENTS, AMONG
WHICH ARE SOME CHOICE FRACTIONAL CURRENCY,
CALIFORNIA QUARTER AND HALF DOLLARS,
WITH OTHER LINES OF GOLD COINS.

———— •·• ————

Which will be Sold by Public Auction at

The Art Rooms of GEORGE W. COLE, 19 East 14th St., New York,

HENRY C. MERRY, Auctioneer,

THURSDAY and FRIDAY, OCTOBER 15 and 16, 1896,

AT TWO O'CLOCK EACH DAY.

————————

The Coins will be on Exhibition from 9.30 A. M. to 1 P. M. each day.

————————

CATALOGUED BY

LYMAN H. LOW,
36 WEST 129th STREET,
NEW YORK, N. Y.

THE SIZE OF

COINS AND MEDALS

In this Catalogue, is given in Millimeters.

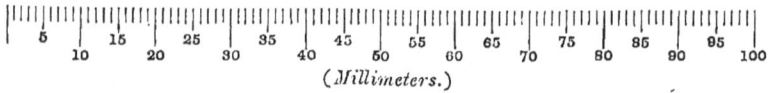

(Millimeters.)

ABBREVIATIONS USED.

abt.	about.	hd.	head.	*Res.*	restrike.
Æ	Copper.	Imp.	Imperial.	Rl.	} Reals.
Æ	Silver.	ins.	inscription.	Rls.	
asst.	{ assorted.	Krzrs.	Kreuzers.	sep.	{ separate.
	{ assortment.	Kop.	Kopecks.		{ separating.
Bai.	Baiocchi.	*l.*	left.	std.	} seated.
bet.	between.	Lib.	Liberty.	setd.	
bril.	brilliant.	Marav.	Maravedis.	Sh.	} Shilling.
bzd.	bronzed.	mil.	military.	Shil.	
Com.	Commemorating.	Mks.	Marks.	shld.	shield.
Conf.	Confederation.	*m. m.*	mint mark.	sim.	similar.
Coron.	Coronation.	mon.	monogram.	Slds.	Sueldos.
Ctvs.	Centavos.	mtd.	mounted.	sq.	square.
CS.	Counterstamp.	n. d.	no date.	stdg.	standing.
Cwn.	Crown.	O.	} Obverse.	sup.	supplement.
cwnd.	crowned.	*Obv.*		sup.	} supported.
d.	pence.	oct.	} octagonal.	suptd.	
dbl.	double.	octag.		Thlr.	Thaler.
dif.	different.	orig.	original.	Trans.	Translation.
do.	ditto.	pc.	piece.	unc.	uncirculated.
Ex.	Exergue.	pf.	proof.	v.	very.
ex.	extra.	Quat.	Quattrini.	var.	{ variety.
Far.	Farthing.	*r.*	right.		{ varieties.
gd.	good.	Rʒ	} Reverse.	W.m.	White metal.
Guld.	Gulden.	*Rev.*		wrth.	wreath.

U. S. Mints are designated as follows: C., Charlotte; C. C., Carson City; D., Dahlonega; O., New Orleans; S., San Francisco; without letter, Philadelphia.

*** All manner of copies and impositions are excluded from my sales.

*** Catalogues of this Sale, priced in red ink, 75 cents.

*** Coin of Alex. III, in lot 36, is a "Drachm" instead of "Didrachm," as printed.

INSTRUCTIONS TO BIDDERS.

Coins and medals are sold so much per piece, U. S. proof sets excepted. You cannot bid for one piece in a lot. If a lot contains ten pieces, and you desire to offer $2 for it, make your bid 20c. The auctioneer will accept an advance of 1 cent up to 50c., then 5c. up to $2.50, when 10c. is the limit, up to $10, and thereafter not less than 25c. Hence any bid up to 50c. can be entertained, but after that the bid must be 55c., 60c., and so on. Such offers as 53c., $1.01, and all intermediate figures are unavailable.

CATALOGUE.

GREEK COPPER.

Autonomous. Amba, Asido, Asido and Astapa, Astapa, Carmo, Gades, Sisapona. Some large. Fair to good.   9

Ana or Ona, Bilbilis, Clunia, Emporia, Iba, Ilerda, Ilerda and Cissa, etc., and Gallia. Some large. Poor to good.   10

Tuder. Sextans. Almond-shaped. Central Italy. Cales, Neapolis, Venusia, Graxa, Tarentum, Thurium. Mostly fair.   12

Bruttium (2), Locri, Vibo, Valentia, Rhegium, Agrigentum (4), Alaesa, Centuripae, Gela, etc. Fair to very good.   15

Syracuse (8), Aphitis, Amphipolis (2), Philippi, Larissa, and Boeotia, etc. Poor to good.   16

Athens (6), Sicyon, Argos (3), Gortyna, Phaestus, Cyros, Amisus (3). Fair to good.   15

Adramyteum, Pergamum, Erythrae, Taba, Apamea, Laodiceia, Antiochia ad Orontem (5), Sidon, etc. Mostly good.   15

Cyrene, Carthago (4), Melita, etc. Mostly above the average size. Poor to good.   14

Duplicates of preceding. Emporia, Neapolis, Athens, Carthago, etc. Poor to good.   15

Regal. Syracuse. Agathocles, Hieron II (2). Macedonia. Alex. III (4), Phil. III (2), Cassander (2). Mostly v. good.   11

Thracia, Lysimachus. Pontus, Rhoemetalces. Syria, Antiochus I, Seleucus II, Demetrius, etc., to Antiochus IX. Mostly very good.   12

Characene, Attambelus. Bactria, Eucratides, Hooerkes, etc. (4). Egypt, Ptol. II to XI (6), etc. Poor to good.   15

4 GREEK SILVER.

13 Duplicates of preceding. Syracuse, Thracia, Bactria, Egypt.
Poor to good. 8

14 **Imperial.** Carthago Nova. Celsa, Ilici, Romula, all with hd
of Augustus, Romula, Segobriga, time of Tiberius. Fair. 6

15 Panormus, Thessalonica, M. Antony, Domitian and wife, Plau-
tina. Very fair. Scarce lot. 4

16 Corinthus, with portraits of Augustus, Caius and Lucius. Nicea,
Mytilene, Germanicus and Agrippina. Smyrna, Laodiceia,
Sabina, etc. Poor to good. 10

17 Antiochia, Phil. I, Macrinus. Anazabus, Caracalla (2), Valerianus. Flaviopolis, Mopsus, Tarsus, M. Aurel. and Treb.
Gallus, etc. Mostly large. Poor to very good. 11

18 Cæsareia, Commodus. Antiochia, Berytus, Hadrian, Elagabalus. Nicibis, Singara, Gord. III and Tranquillina. Size of
first and second bronze. Poor to very good. 6

19 Alexandria. Agrippina, Claudius, Nero and Poppaea, Acquillia
Severa, Maximiamus, Tranquillina, Quietus, etc. Some are
large. Poor to very good. 13

20 Judaea. Pontius Pilatus, A. D. 35-36. Simpulum. ℞ Three
ears of corn bound together. Very fair. 1

21 Simon Bar-Cochab, A. D. 132-135. Palm tree. ℞ Vine leaf.
Very fair. 1

GREEK SILVER.

22 **Autonomous.** Gallia. ℞ Horse, wheel above. Very good.
Size 13. Massilia. Good. 17. Phistelia. Fine. 10. 3

23 Metapontum. Barley head. ℞ Incuse. Good. 11. Also
Didrachm, with hd of Persephone. Very fair. 2

24 Thurium, B. C. 390-350. Pallas hd *r.* ℞ Bull butting *r.*, fish
below. Very good, *obv.* fine. Didr. 20. 1

25 Croton, B. C. 550-480. Tripod. ℞ Incuse of *obv.* Good,
thick. 18. 1

26 B. C. 330-299. Eagle on olive branch, wings spread. ℞ ΚΡΟ.
Tripod, crane *r.* Stater. Rare type. Nearly fine. 1

27 Agrigentum. Fair. 14. Thracian Chers. Good. 13. By-
zantium. Fair. 9. 3

28 Gela, B. C. 466-415. CEVAΣ. (*sic.*) Forepart of man-headed
bull *r.* ℞ Armed horseman galloping *r.* Didr. Very good.
Nearly fine. 20. 1

0 29 Thasos, B. C. 465–411. Seilenos carrying off struggling nymph.
℞ Quadripartite square. Stater. Very good. 21.   1

5 30 Istrus, B. C. 300. Two hds united, one reversed. ℞ IΣTPIH.
Sea eagle on dolphin. Drachm. Very good. 17.   1

31 Pharsalus. Horse's head. 14. Apollonia. 16. Histiæa, var.
13 and 15. Good to fine.   5

32 Athens. 12. Argos. 13. Both v. good. Phaestus and others
unidentified. Poor. 10 to 12.   5

33 Chius, B. C. 330–300. Apollo head *r*. ℞ (ΔHMH) | TPIOΣ.
Magistrate's name and prow. Hemidrachm. Fine. 13.   1

34 Apollonia ad Rhyndacum, B. C. 400–330. Anchor and lob-
ster. ℞ Gorgon hd. Good. 14. Parium. Gorgon hd.
℞ Bull looking back. Fine, though *rev*. not well centered.
13.   2

35 Miletus. Lion's head. ℞ Floral star. Good. 9. Cnidus.
Lion's hd. ℞ Aphrodite hd in incuse square. Nearly fine.
Thick drachm. 15.   2

36 **Regal.** Phil. II. Apollo hd *r*. ℞ Youth on horse. Tetro-
bol. Nearly fine. 14. Alex. III. Heracles hd in lion's
skin. Dıdr. Fine. 17.   2

37 Cappadocia, Ariarthes, B. C. 130–100. Ariobarzanes I, B. C.
93–59. Drachms with King's hd. Good. 16, 17.   2

38 Syria. Demetrius I, B. C. 162–151. Drachm. Good. 17.   1-

39 Demetrius II, B. C. 146–126. His hd *r*. ℞ Ptolemaic eagle.
Good. *Obv*. not well centered. Tetradrachm.   1-

40 Antiochus VIII, B. C. 121–96. ℞ Zeus seated holds star and
sceptre. Tetr. Very good.   1

41 Parthia. Phraates IV, B. C. 37–2. Bust *l*. ℞ Tyche offers
wrth to setd monarch. Tetr. *Obv*. fine, *rev*. very good.   1

42 Persia. Darius I, B. C. 521–486. The King with bow and
arrow, kneeling. ℞ Irregular oblong incuse. Siglos. Thick.
Very good. Oval 13 x 15.   1

43 A variety of last, body much larger. V. fair. Also, Parthian
Drachm of Orodes I. Good.   2

44 **Imperial.** Caesareia. Germanicus, who made it a Roman
Province, Claudius and Nero, Trajan, Ant. Pius. Alexandria.
Nero and Tiberius, Nero and Poppaea. 2 Denarii, others
are potin Tetradrachms. Good. Scarce lot.   6

ROMAN CONSULAR BRONZE.

45 Aelia, Asinia, both "Ob civis servatos" type. Canidia, Livineia, Maecilia, Nonia, and Salvia. S. B. to G. B. Only one poor.   7

46 Opeimia, Pinaria, Trebonia, and others, Roma. Semis 5, Aes 3. Poor to very good.   8

ROMAN IMPERIAL SMALL BRONZE.

47 Tiberius, Caligula, Claudius, Nero, Domitian (3 types), Trajan (2 types). Good to fine.   9

48 Gallienus (4), Salonina, Claudius II (3), Quintillus (2), Aurelian, Val. and Aurelian (poor), Postumus, Victorinus (2), Tetricus I (2). Good to fine.   17

49 Gallienus (4), Claud. II (2), Quintillus (2), Postumus, Victorinus, Tetricus I and II (2), Licinius I, Carus (3, one Divo Caro Pio). Good to fine.   17

50 Tetricus I and II (2), Carus, Carinus (3), Numerianus (2), Diocletian (2), Maximianus I (2, one with Hercules and lion), Carausius, Allectus, Constantius I, Licinius II (2). Two poor, others mostly fine.   18

51 Carinus (2), Numerianus (2), Diocletian, Maximianus I, Licinius II (2), Constantine I, Fausta, Crispus (2), Helena (mother of Constantine) 2. Two poor, others good to fine.   17

52 Magnia Urbica (supposed wife of Carinus), MAGNIA VRBICA AVG. Bust *r.* ℞ VENUS GENETRIX. *Obv.* very good, *rev.* good. Every letter distinct. Size 21. Very rare. Valued from 30 to 50 Fcs.   1

53 Constantine I, Fausta, Crispus, Constantine II, Constans, Magnentius, Constantius II, Julian II, with varieties of some. Good to fine.   17

54 Theodora (second wife of Constantius I). ℞ PIETAS ROMANA. Nearly fine, rare.   1

55 Another of Theodora. Fair. Jovianus, Honorius. ℞ Emperor mtd. Very good. Scarce lot.   3

56 Delmatius. ℞ Two soldiers stdg, between them a military standard. *Ex.* S M A L D. Very fine, rare.   1

57 Another. Sim. with dif. bust. S M K L in *ex.* Very fair, rare.   1

58 Helena (wife of Julian), Valentinian I (3), Valens, Gratianus, Theodosius (2), Honorius, Arcadius (3). Fair to v. good. 12
59. Victor, son of Maximus II. ℞ SPES ROMANORUM. Open gate of camp. Very fine and rare. 1
60 Eudoxia (wife of Theodosius II). Her bust *r.* *Obv.* v. good, *rev.* barely fair. Very rare. 1
61 Marcianus, husband of Pulcheria. His bust *r.* ℞ Monogram within wrth. Quinarius size. V. good and the rarest S. B. in this collection. 1

SECOND BRONZE.

62 Augustus, Agrippa, Tiberius, Antonia, Drusus, Germanicus. Excellent portraits. Good and very good. 6
63 Others. Augustus, Agrippa, Tiberius, Germanicus, Caligula, Claudius, Nero. Fair to good. 7
64 Others, still varying. Augustus, Livia, Caligula, Claudius, the latter handsomely patinated. Good. 4
65 Nero, Vespasian, Domitian (℞ The Emperor mtd), Nerva, Trajan, Hadrian, Aelius. Poor to good. 7
66 Nero, Domitian (rare *rev.*, three figures sacrificing), Hadrian, Ant. Pius, Faustina I and II. Fair to very good. 7
67 Galba. ℞ S. C. Roman eagle between two standards. Rare type. Good. 1
68 Julia (daughter of Titus). Bust and most of legend fairly preserved. *Rev.* very poor. Extremely rare. 1
69 Domitian, Trajan, Hadrian, Sabina, Aelius, Ant. Pius, Faustina I, Commodus. Fair to good. 7
70 Trajan (2 types, nearly fine), Ant. Pius, Faustina I and II, Commodus. Good. 6
71 Lucilla (good, beautifully patinated), Crispina (nearly fine), Septimus Severus (good), Geta (with rare *rev.*, poor). 4
72 Commodus, M. Aurel., Aurelian (3), Postumus, Tacitus, Probus, varieties of some. Poor to good. 10
73 Aurelian (2), Tacitus, Probus (4), Diocletian (2), Maximianus I (2), Constantius I. Good to fine. 12
74 Aurelian (2), Tacitus, Probus (3), Diocletian (2), Constantius I, Maximianus II, Maximinus II. Good to fine. 16
75 Severina. ℞ IVNO REGINA. Nearly fine, rare. 1

76 Severina (a slight variety of last, v. fair), Florianus, Probus (2),
   Maximianus I, Constantius I (2), Maximianus II, Maximinus
   II (2). Good to fine.   10

77 Diocletian, Maximianus II, Maxentius, Constantine I, Constantius II, Decentius, Julian II, Valentinian, varieties of two.
   Good to fine.   10

78 Valeria (daughter of Diocletian). R̸ VENERI VICTRICI. Fine
   and rare.   1

79 Severus II, Maxentius, Constantine I (2), Constantius II, Constans, Magnentius, Decentius, Constantius Gallus, Theodosius, Arcadius, Honorius. Mostly good to fine.   12

80 Romulus. R̸ AETERNAE MEMORIA. A temple. Very fair and
   rare.   1

81 Gratianus (2), Magnus Maximus, Valentinian II (rare), Theodosius (2), Arcadius (2), Honorius (2). Good.   10

82 Valentinian II (good), Flacilla (very fair). Both rare.   2

FIRST BRONZE.

83 Tiberius, (OB | CIVES | SER within wrth type). Poor. All
   others that follow are with portrait. Claudius, Agrippina.
   Good.   3

84 Drusus. R̸ Claudius std. V. good. Fields retouched.   1

85 Nero, Vespasian, Nerva, Trajan. Fair to good.   4

86 Vespasian. R̸ JVDAEA CAPTA. Very fair.   1

87 Vespasian. R̸ CAES. AVG. F. DESIG. etc. Titus and Domitian
   stdg in military habit. Struck A. D. 71. Very good, rare.
   Cohen, 20 fcs.   1

88 Titus, Domitian, Trajan. Good and very good.   3

89 Hadrian. R̸ RESTITVTORI ORBIS TERRARVM. V. fair. Sabina.
   V. poor. Aelius. Fair. Ant. Pius. V. good.   4

90 Ant. Pius. R̸ TEMPLVM DIV. etc. Statue of Augustus and
   Livia in temple front. Struck A. D. 159. Good, well patinated, scarce.   1

91 Ant. Pius (3 types), Faustina I, M. Aurel., Faustina II, L.
   Verus. Fair and very fair.   8

92 Faustina I. R̸ VENERI AVGVSTAE. Scarce, nearly fine. M.
   Aurel. Good. L. Verus. Fine, but deeply pitted in several
   places.   3

SILVER DENARII.

93 Faustina I, M. Aurel., Faustina II, (℞ MATRI CASTRORVM, and another), Lucilla (2), Commodus (2), Crispina. Mostly very fair. 9

94 Faustina II. ℞ Peacock. Lucilla, Commodus (3), Sept. Severus (3), Julia Domna. Mostly fair, some good. 9

95 Manlia Scantilla. ℞ Juno stdg. Poor, but rare. Clodius Albinus. Very fair. 2

96 Clodius Albinus. *Obv.* very good. Sept. Severus. ℞ Two victories holding buckler. Fair, scarce. 2

97 Caracalla. ℞ SECVRITATI, etc. V. good. *Obv.* nearly fine. Macrinus. *Obv.* very fair. Julia Soemias. Fair. 3

98 Caracalla (2). Julia Maesa. ℞ Piety stdg. Sev. Alex. (3). Fair to good. 6

99 Sev. Alex. (2), Julia Mamaea, Maximianus I (4). Mostly good. 7

100 Barbia Orbiana. ℞ Concordia std. Rather poor, but rare. 1

101 Pupienus. ℞ Victory stdg. V. good. Planchet cracked from edge to profile. Rare. 1

102 Gord. III (2), Phil. I (2), Otacilia Severa, Phil. II (2), Traj. Decius. Mostly fair to very good. 8

103 Gord. III (2), Phil. I (2), Hostilianus, Treb. Gallus, Volusianus, Valerianus, Postumus. Four poor, others fair to good. 8

104 Traj. Decius, Etruscilla, Herr. Etruscus. ℞ Mercury stdg. Very good, except *Rev.* of last; scarce lot. 3

105 Hostilianus. ℞ PRINCIPI IVVENTVTIS. Good, rare. 1

106 Volusianus. ℞ Statue of Juno within Temple. V. gd., rare. 1

107 Valerianus. ℞ VIRTVS AVGG. V. good, scarce. Postumus. V. fair. *Obv.* about good. 2

108 Mariniana. ℞ CONSECRATIO. Peacock with tail spread. Poor, but very rare. 1

SILVER DENARII.

109 **Consular.** Aquilia, Aurelia, Caecilia (2), Calpurnia, Carisia, Cassia (2), Cornelia, Decimia, Flavia, Flaminia. Several interesting types. Good to fine, mostly of latter. 13

110 Cordia, conjoined hds of the Dioscuri. ℞ Venus stdg., holds balance. Cupid on her shoulder. Good. *Obv.* not well centred. Rare. 1

111 Herennia, M. Her. carrying his father; Licinia, Lucretia, Nep-
     tune hd. ℞ Cupid astride a bridled dolphin. Mamilia. ℞
     Ulysses and his dog Argus, Marcia (3 types, one with hd of
     Ancus, fourth King of Rome), Memmia, Minucia (2 types).
     Good to fine.   10

112 Licinia, Venus hd *r*. ℞ P CRASSVS (M. F.) Soldier beside
     horse. *Rev.* not well centred. Fine and rare.   1

113 Nonia. SVFENAS S. C. Saturn's hd *r*. ℞ SEX NONI (PR. L. V)
     P. F. *Rev.* imperfectly centred. Nearly fine. Rare.   1

114 Norbana, Papia (2 types, 1 with wolf on *rev.*, scarce), Plancia,
     (℞ Goat, scarce), Pompeia (by Sextus Pom., only fair but
     rare), Roscia, Rustia, Servilia, Tituria, Valeria, Vibia, and
     Roma, (3, one with deified Rome std on buckler). Mostly
     very good.   14

115 Publicia, helmeted hd *r*., mallet above. ℞ Pompey the Great
     stdg on prow of galley. Good. *Rev.* fair.   1

116 Pomponia. L. POMPON . MOLO. ℞ Altar bet. male figures and
     goat. Portia, quinarius. Both about good, neither perfectly
     centred.   2

117 Postumia. Diana hd *r*. ℞ A POST. Togated man, bull and
     altar. Fine and rare.   1

118 Procilia, Jupiter hd *r*. ℞ L . PROCILI. F. Juno Sospita stdg
     r. with lance and buckler. Thoria J(uno) S(ospita) M (agna)
     R(egina). Her hd *r*. V. good, both rare.   2

IMPERIAL DENARII.

119 Julius Caesar. 2d Dictatorship, B. C. 48. Head of Ceres.
     M. Antony, B. C. 43–42. ℞ Lion. About good.   2

120 Julius Caesar. Perpetual Dictator, B. C. 44. CAESAR DICT
     PERPETVO. His hd *r*., veiled. Sepullius moneyer. About
     good.   1

121 M. Antony. B. C. 41. His hd *r*. ℞ Hd of Octavius. V.
     good.   1

122 Augustus. Hd. *l*. ℞ Round temple. Hd *r*. ℞ SIGNIS
     RECEPTIS. A buckler bet. standards. Both B. C. 20. The
     latter rare. V. fair and good.   2

123 Augustus. Fair. Tiberius. Tribute penny. Good. Nero.
     Poor.   3

124 Tiberius. His hd *r*. ℞ The emperor in quadriga, *r*. Struck
     A. D. 15. Fine.   1
125 Caligula. His hd *r*. ℞ Hd of Augustus bet. stars.   Struck
     A. D. 37. Corroded. Edges chipped, otherwise good.
     Vespasian. V. good. Titus. ℞ Sow *l*. Good.   3
126 Nero. ℞ SA—LV(S). Health setd *l*. Fine, and although not
     a well circled planchet, as few are, its equal is rarely met
     with.   1
127 Galba. ℞ Victory on globe. Very good, scarce.   1
128 Vitellius. ℞ Tripod. Very good, scarce.   1
129 Vitellius. ℞ Concordia std. Vespasian. ℞ Vase, simpulum,
     etc. Titus. V. good.   3
130 Titus. ℞ Burning Altar. Restoration by Gallienus. Cor-
     roded and bent, otherwise good.   Domitian (2). Nerva,
     Trajan (2), Hadrian (2). V. good to nearly fine.   8
131 Sabina (2), Aelius. ℞ Veiled female sacrificing (scarce).
     Ant. Pius. V. good to nearly fine.   4
132 Ant. Pius, Faustina I (2), M. Aurel. (2), Faustina II (2), L.
     Verus, Lucilla (2). V. good to fine.   10
133 Lucilla, Commodus, Crispina, Sept. Severus, Julia Domna,
     Caracalla, Geta (2), Elagabalus (2). Good to fine.   10
134 Clodius Albinus.   ℞ Roma victrix std. Good, rare.   1
135 Plautilla, Macrinus, Julia Paula. (℞ Concordia std. Rare).
     Good to fine.   3
136 Julia Soaemias, Julia Maesa, Sev. Alex. (2), Julia Mamaea,
     Maximianus I, Gord. III (2), Phil. I, Otacilia Severa. Good
     to fine.   10
137 Barbia Orbiana. ℞ Concordia std. Good, very rare.   1
138 Balbinus. ℞ Two hands joined. V. good. Rare.   1
139 Otacilia Severa. ℞ Concordia std. Phil. II. ℞ The Em-
     peror stdg. Both scarce. Traj. Decius (2), Etruscilla.
     Good to fine.   5
140 Herenninus Etruscus, Treb. Gallus, Volusianus, Valerianus (2),
     Gallienus, Salonina.   Mostly fine, several scarce reverses.   7
141 Mariniana. ℞ CONSECRATIO. Mariniana borne by peacock
     in full flight. Good, very rare.   1
142 Saloninus (2). (One with *rev.* eagle flying bearing Saloninus.
     Rare).   Claud. II, Aurelianus, Severina, Postumus (2),
     Victorinus, Tacitus. All base silver. Good to fine.   9

143 Tetricus II. ℞ (Princ. Jv)vent.   The Prince of youth stdg.
     Obv. V. fair. *Rev.* poor.   Of good silver and very rare.   1
144 Florianus (scarce), Probus, Carinus, Numerianus, Diocletian.
     All base, with a dup. of Hadrian and Gord. III.   Good to
     very fine.   7
145 Maximianus I. ℞ virtvs militvm.   Four soldiers sacrificing
     before the Praetorian Camp. Fine, rare.   1
146 Constantius I. ℞ Type of last. Fine, rare.   1
147 Maximianus II. ℞ Type of last. Fine, rare.   1
148 Licinius I, Constantine I, (both base), Constantius II, Julian
     II. Good to nearly fine.   4
149 Valentinian I. V. good. Valens. Fine. Arcadius. Fair.   3
150 Gratianus, Honorius, Arcadius. Good and very good.   3
151 Theodosius I, Arcadius. V. good.   2

BYZANTINE, ETC.

152 *Small to large brass.* Anastasius I, A. D. 491 to Manuel II,
     1425, representing upwards of forty-five reigns, among which
     are specimens of the Gothic and Vandal Kings.   All named.
     Poor to fine, fewest of last.   74
153 *Silver.* Justinianus, Athalaricus, and Heracleus. Fine. Sizes
     14, 11, 10.   3
154 Constans II (with three associates), Constantius Pogonat,
     Heracleus and Tiberius, Johannes II (2 var.), Manuel I,
     Johannes III and IV. An unusual lot.   Good to fine.
     20 to 22.   6
155 Duplicates of Byzantine, and poor small to large brass.
     Roman Imperial and Byzantine (including cup shapes)
     with Silver Coins of Roman Rep. (3), Byzantine (1). Many
     are fair to good.   53

AMERICAN COLONIAL.

156 1722. Rosa Americana penny. Good. Heavily corroded.
     Vermontensium, 1786. Good. *Rev.* fair. 1788. Bust.
     Very good.   3
157 Massachusetts. 1787. Cent. Fine, but corroded.   1
158 Connecticut. 1785, '86, '87, '88. Cents. Very good. Two
     nearly fine.   4

159 New York. 1787. Nova Eborac. 1789. Mott's Token.
1794. Talbot, A. and L. New Jersey. 1786. Virginia.
1773. Fair to good.   5
160 New Jersey. 1787. Cent. Maris 73aa, who states that the
three he has seen were struck over Connecticut cents. This
is the case with this specimen, and it is far superior to the
one represented on his plate. The *obv.* legend reads clearly
CONNEC : LURIBUS ✚ UNUM ✚ ℞ ETLIB : CÆSAREA ✚ . .
Rarity. 5.   1
161 Nova Constelatio. 1783. Constellatio. 1785. Fugio. 1787.
United States. Good.   3
162 Washington. 1783. Unity Cent. Nearly fine. Also with
United States, a restrike. V. fine. Dbl hd cent. Georgivs
Triumpho, and small Success. V. fair.   5

HARD TIMES TOKENS.

163 ANDREW JACKSON. Hd *r.* ℞ THE BANK MUST PERISH. Within wrth, THE UNION MUST AND SHALL BE PRESERVED. Low
1. Fine. In white metal. Size 28½.   1

I have never seen but one other in this metal, although I am told of two, and
there are possibly more. If so, they have successfully eluded earnest pursuit for
more than twelve years.

164 Another as last, but in copper. Somewhat dented and holed,
but by no means is it a bad specimen. Size 27.   1
165 FOR THE CONSTITUTION HURRA ! Ship *l.* ℞ FLOURISH COM-
MERCE' etc. Low 2. Uncirculated, and unlike all others
that have passed through my hands, it has a plain edge.
Rare and especially valuable in such condition.   1
166 THE GLORIOUS WHIG VICTORY OF 1834. Liberty cap on rays.
℞ FELLOW CITIZENS SAVE YOUR CONSTITUTION. Ship *r.*
Low 3. Fine. Size 26½. In white metal and of great rarity,
and scarcely less valuable than No. 1 in the same metal.
Both are wonderful strangers to me.   1
167 Others. Boar running. Low 4. Jackson stdg. Low 8, also
16, 21, 22, 25, 39, 50, 52. Good to fine.   9
168 Hd *l.* ℞ LBENTONIAN etc. L. 43. Fine.   1
169 Liberty hd. ℞ Dayton's card. L. 61. Fine.   1

170   Liberty hd *l.* ℞ Centre Market. L. 66. Unc., many parts
        bright.   1
171   Abraham Riker. ℞ Millions for Defence. L. 70. V. fine,
        some original red.   1
172   Others. L. 64 (poor), 65, 74, 78, 79, 86, 90, 92. Mostly fine.   8

The following cards bearing dates from 1833 to '37 are numbered according
to the arrangement I have made for a second edition of my Hard Times Tokens,
the preparation of which was begun more than a year ago, and which will, I trust,
be completed some time during 1897. The classification and descriptions are fin-
ished (numbering 157), but the search for historical notes which I aim to have
accompany the series, together with the determining of the makers and their mints,
is causing much unexpected delay. Already I have secured valuable data, much
never before known to the collecting fraternity. But to gather now what might
and should have been harvested thirty-five years ago is a task, though an interesting one, attended with considerable labor. I introduce the subject through this
note, believing it fitting and opportune by reason of the gems found in the collection herein offered, which make up some of the most substantial parts of the
new story.

173   1833. Hathaway, Fall River. 74. Robinson's, Jones & Co.,
        N. Y. 76. 1834. W. A. Handy, Prov. 78. H. M. & E.
        I. Richards, Attleboro. 83. 1835. Bucklin, Troy. 92.
        Walsh's, Lansingburgh. 99. 1837. Anderson, N. Y. 107.
        Benedict & Burnham, Waterbury. 109. Size, Portsmouth.
        131. Smith, Dover. 132. Good to fine, chiefly of latter.   10
174   1836. HUCKEL, BURROWS & JENNINGS — DEALERS | IN | GRO-
        CERIES CHOICE WINES | &C &C. ℞ BOAT STORES | AND | SHIP
        CHANDLERY | MAIN STREET | ST LOUIS. 102. Brass, 29. V.
        fine and of the highest rarity.   1

This card was wanting in the Levick collection, and I can find it in but a
single catalogue during the last 18 years, and that had "Huckel" erased. I do
not know of another perfect specimen.

175   1837. NATHAN. C. FOLGER. — NEW ORLEANS   In field, DEALER
        IN | READY MADE | etc., in 7 lines. ℞ BOYS AND | CHIL-
        DREN'S CLOTHING | etc. 1837, in 7 lines; by *Bale & Smith.*
        121. Slightly damaged on *rev.,* otherwise nearly fine. Size
        34. Found only in the Levick sale, where it brought $11.25.   1
176   1837. Smith's Clock Establishment, N. Y. 136. Unc., most
        parts bright.   1
177   Wolfe, Clark & Spies, N. Y. Bust of Washington *r.,* in oval.
        ℞ Bust of Jackson in oval. Holed and rather poor, but
        very rare.   1

178 Wolfe, Spies & Clark, N. Y. Bust of Washington *r.*, in oval.
     ℞ N. Y. Grand Canal opened, 1823. Fine and of the high-
     est order of rarity in the series of Store Cards or Washing-
     tons.   1
179 Treadwell, Kissam & Co. ℞ As last. J. & L. Brewster, by
     Bale. Buchan, *Northmore* St., and Richardson, 104 Market
     St., Phila. Good to fine. All brass.   4
180 Other Cards of the period. Boston, Fair Haven, Troy, New
     York, Phila., *Racim*, Grand Rapids, Chicago, St. Louis, etc.,
     includes the large California Token, 1849 Steamship with
     flag above. Good to fine.   34
181 Duplicate Cards, Tokens, etc., includes a fine Treadwell, Kis-
     sam & Co. Good to fine.   17
182 War Tokens. Pittsburgh, Alleghany City, Cinn., Detroit, Chi-
     cago and various small places in the West, together with a
     larger assortment of N. Y. City, and others, with busts, pop-
     ular war cries, industrial emblems, etc. A fine lot.   155

UNITED STATES.

183 **Half Cents.** 1793 Dark chocolate shade. V. fine.   1
184 1794 Very good.   1
185 1800 Fair. '04 V. fine. '05 Good. '06 No stems. Fine.   4
186 1803 Very fine ; rare in this condition.   1
187 1807, '08, '09, '10 (fair), '25, '26, '28. Good to unc., sharp. 7
188 1829 Unc., red.   1
189 1832 Unc., dark olive. '33 Very fine.   2
190 1834 (2), '35, '49, '51, '53 to '57. Mostly fine.   11
191 **Cents.** 1793 Vine and bars. More corroded than worn. V.
     fair.   1
192 1794 Hays 17. V. fine. Slight evidences of wear. Some
     corrosion on *obv.* and *rev.* Light reddish color.   1
193 1794 Hays 11, Good. H. 45, Fine, edge clipped to top of Lib.
     cap. H. 54, Very good.   3
194 1795 One Cent high in wreath, also in centre. '96 Lib. cap.
     Very fair.   3
195 1797, '98, 2 var. of each. 1800, '01, '02. Fair.   7
196 1799 Poor. Last two figures of date show fairly well. Rare. 1
197 1802 Without stems to wreath. Very good.   1

198	1803 Small and large $\frac{1}{100}$. V. good, nearly fine. '06 Fair.	3
199	1805 Very good, a little less than fine.	1
200	1807 over '06. Fair. Perfect date. Good. '08 The so-called 12 stars. Fair. 13 stars, nearly fine, dark.	4
201	1809 Very fair.	1
202	1810 Perfect date, darkest green. '12 Small and large date. '14 Plain and crosslet 4. Good to nearly fine.	5
203	1811 over '10. Very fair. '13 Very good.	2
204	1811 Perfect date. Very good.	1
205	1816 Fine, medium olive.	1
206	1817 Very fine, mostly red, also 15 stars, very fair.	2
207	1817 Vars. of the 13 stars class. Good.	4
208	1818, '19, 2 vars. of each (includes '19 over '18). Good to fine, partly bright.	4
209	1820 over '19, good; and perfect date, unc., red. Some discoloration on *obv*.	2
210	1821, '22 (2 vars.), '24, '25. Very good.	5
211	1823 Perfect date. V. good, considerably above those commonly met with.	1
212	1826, '27, '28 (large date), '29. Good to v. good, one nearly fine.	4
213	1830 Circle within milling around border. Uncirculated, light olive, portions red; a rare gem. Few cabinets equal, none excel.	1
214	1830 Without the inner circle. Various cuts on edge not reaching surface of *obv*. or *rev*., slightest marks of circulation, reddish; desirable.	1
215	1831, '32 (fine, dark), '33. Good.	3
216	1834 Sm. date. Good. Large do., with large letters. Fair. '35 Sm. and large date. V. good, and good.	4
217	1837 Plain hair cord. Unc., light olive and red.	1
218	1836, '37, and '39 with head of '38, and Silly and Booby hds. Good.	5
219	1838 Unc., except for a few slight blemishes; at least half red.	1
220	1839 With hd of '40. Unc., medium olive; in this condition rare and very desirable.	1
221	1840 (small and large date), '41, '43. Good.	4
222	1842 Small date. Nearly fine, dark. Large do. Very fine, light olive.	2

223	1844 Nearly fine. '45 Fine.	2
224	1846 Low, medium and high dates. 2 good, 1 fine.	3
225	1847 Unc., *obv.* mostly red.	1
226	1848 Fine, some red on *rev.* '52 About unc., light olive.	2
227	1849, '50, '51, '55, 56. Fine.	5
228	1853, '54, '55 (straight '55). Unc., most parts bright.	3
229	1857 Small date. Fine.	1
230	1857 Large date. Fine.	1
231	Others. 1793 Chain, poor, and holed through date. Also wrth var., date recognizable. '94 (3), '95 (2), '98, 1800, '01 (3 each). Mostly poor.	17
232	1802 (5), '03 (6), '05, '07 (2), '10 (2), '12, '13, '14 (2). Poor to good, one holed.	20
233	1816 to '56, excepting '21, '39, '46. Poor to fine, the intermediate prevailing.	79
234	Set of Cents 1793 to 1856, lacking '96, '99, 1804, '06, '09, '39. The '93 is the chain var., poor but everything visible. Few poor or fine, mostly fair and good.	57
235	**Trimes.** 1852, '62. Fine. Three Cents, nickel, '79. Proof, cheek rubbed. Also 20 Cents, 1875, S. mint. About unc.	4
236	**Half Dimes.** 1795 V. fair. 1830, '32 to '35, '37 (starless), '57, '58, '63, '67. Mostly fine and unc.	11
237	1800 The LIBEKTY var. Very fine, two slight edge dents, *obv.* and *rev.*	1
238	**Dimes.** 1807 V. fair. '21, '25, '27, '29. Fair to good.	5
239	1820 Large date. V. fine. '34 Unc.	2
240	1835, '37 (starless), '38 (O. and P. mints), '53 (arrows), '64, '67, '73 (without arrows), '77 (C.C.), '79. Mostly very fine and unc.	10
241	**Quarter Dolls.** 1796 V. good, worn much less than usual; scarce.	1
242	1805, '06. Very good.	2
243	1805, '06, each with a duplicate, and vars. of last. Good.	4
244	1807 Extremely fine, slight scratch below L in Liberty, otherwise but trifling marks of circulation, a rare state of preservation.	1
245	1818 Nearly fine. '19 Attempted puncture. Very good.	2
246	1818 (var. of *rev.* of last), '20. Both very good.	2
247	1821 Very fine.	1

248 1825, '28 Very good.   2
249 1839 Extremely fine, a trifle less than unc.   1
250 1862, '73 (no arrows, fine), '74 (S. mint), '79. Slight marks
       of circulation.   4
251 **Half Dollars.** 1795 Good.   1
252 1803 Very fair. '06 Very good.   2
253 1805 over '04. Very good, light scratches above o in date.   1
254 1806 Very fine, some original lustre.   1
255 1812 Very fair. '14 Fine. '21 About good.   3
256 1825, '28. Nearly fine.   2
257 1831 V. good. '33 Very fine. '36 Very good.   3
258 **Dollars.** 1795 Head. Nearly fine. Slight break in die
       behind hd. 5 in date lightly scratched.   1
259 1795 A var. of last, about its equal in condition.   1
260 1795 Bust. Good, dent on edge.   1
261 1796 Large date. Good.   1
262 1798 Large eagle. Fine. Some light nicks, and weak about
       eagle's hd.   1
263 1798 A var. of last. Very good.   1
264 1799 Very good.   1
265 1800 Nearly fine.   1
266 1803 Large 3. Good, two light scratches on neck.   1
267 1842 Good.   1

FOREIGN COPPER.

268 Canada. 1813 Trade and Navigation Farthing. Very good,
       rare.   1
269 Speed the Plough. Carritt & Alport, Nova Scotia Half Cent,
       etc., with Edward Stephens, 1816 Penny Token, included by
       Sandham. Good, a few fine.   11
270 Mexico, Honduras, Barbadoes, Danish W. I., Santa Marta,
       Caracas, Spanish Guiana, etc. 1 duplicate, mostly good.   30
270a England. Styca of Eanred 808–840. Fine. 13.   1
271 Chas. II, 1675 ¼ and ½d (the latter rare); Wm. and Mary, ¼
       and ½d, also ¼d. of Wm. III, Geo. I and II, with others to
       Vic. V. fair to good.   13
272 Geo. III, 1797, the large 2 Penny piece. Fine, a few light
       nicks.   1
273 Wm. IV, 1831 Penny. Very fine, uncommon in this condition.   1

274 Ireland. Eliz., 1601 Halfpenny. V. fair, rare. Jas. I, Far. Good, *rev.* imperfectly centred. 2
275 Jas. II, 1689 Novbr. Shil. 1690 Cwn, Gun money, also ½d 1685 and Wm. III do. 1696, etc. 1 poor, others good. 5
276 Scotland. Wm. III, 1696 2d. Poor. Guernesey, Jersey and Isle of Man. Good. 5
277 Isle of Man. George III, 1813, Penny. Very fine, medium olive. 1
278 Norway. Fred. VI, 1811 to Chas. XV, 1867. Sweden. Chas. XII, 1708 to Oscar II, 1881, including 3 Baron De Gortz Dalers. 2 fair, others good to fine. 28
279 Denmark. Chris. VII, 1771 to Chris. IX, 1874. Gd to fine. 12
280 Artois, Brabant, Campen, Frisia, Utrecht, etc. Mostly early. Poor to good. 16
281 Antwerp, 1814. Lille, 1708. Both siege pieces. Holland, Belgium, Liege. Poor to unc. 12
282 France. Hy IV, Louis XIV, etc. to Nap. III, including siege of Mayence, 5 Sols, and issues for the Colonies. A few poor, others good to fine. 25
283 Spain. Ferd. and Is., Phil. III, IV, Chas. II, Phil. V, Chas. III, to Rep. 1870. Poor to fine. 22
284 Cities and Provinces in Spain. Bellpuig? Barcelona, (1 Quarto,) Majorca, Segovia? All scarce or rare. Also Portugal, John VI. Poor to good. 12
285 German States and Cities. Aachen, Bocholt, Munster, Oldenburg, etc. Also Hungary and Austria. Mostly good to fine. 26
286 Italy. Milan, Papal, Parthenopian Rep., Vicenza, Sicily, etc. Several early. Scarce or rare. Poor to fine. 25
287 Russia. Peter the Great, Cath. I, Anna, Peter III (2 Kop., scarce) to Alex. III. Generally good to fine. 20
288 Turkey, Armenia, Greece, Malta, Egypt, Morocco, Liberia, St. Helena, Madeira. Good to fine. 15
289 Oran. Phil. III, 4 Maravedis. Arms, IIII. ℞ o | RA | N. Fair and rare. Not recorded in Scott's catalogue. 1
290 India, Bengal, Madras, Dutch Indies, Straits, Cambodia (Att, a hen *l.* F. 2156. V. rare), Japan, etc. 22
291 Tokens, etc. England. Halfpenny Tokens. Conder period, chiefly 1788-96. Several scarce or rare, mostly very fine. 32

292 Halfpenny Tokens. Another assortment, all different from preceding and in same condition. 32

293 A third assortment, same condition. 32

294 A fourth assortment, in same condition. 26

295 The remainder of the collection of Halfpennies. Poor and fair. 11. Farthings. 8. Mostly fine, 2 very rare. 19

296 English and Irish Farthing Tokens of present Century. Also Edward Kent, 1668 and Sherborn Farthing, 1669. Good to fine. 35

297 Others of present Century. Halfpennies, 12. Pennies, 16 (including one of 1787). Chiefly good to fine. 28

298 Money weights, Abbey pieces, Counters, Jetons and Spielmarks, 18th and 19th Centuries, and some earlier, including Counters of Anne and Geo. II (described in M. I., Anne 277 and Geo. II, 20) ; of the latter it is there stated that no specimen has been met with. Good to fine. 56

299 Medalets and Jetons. Coronation, Political, Temperance, Mortuary and Religious, chiefly English. Good to fine. 33

300 **Base Coins.** W. I. Islands, Low Countries and Swiss Cantons. Many fine, some early, a few large. 33

301 German States and Cities, Italy, Turkey, etc., 16th to 19th Centuries. 5 duplicates. Good to fine. 73

FOREIGN SILVER.

302 Mexico. Chas. and Joanna, 2 Rls; Phil. II, do. Fair. Ferd. VI, 1 and 2 Rls. Good. 4

303 Chas. III, 2 Rls ; Chas. IV, Ferd. VII. and Augustin, $\frac{1}{2}$ Rls. Good, also $\frac{1}{4}$ Rl, 1801 Castle type. Fine. 5

304 Chas. III, 1787 8 Rls. Bust type. Very good. 1

305 Chas. IV, 1799 8 Rls. Very fine. 1

306 Ferd. VII, Rl (*Revolution* 1810–15). Bust *r*. F–7. ℞ Crowned Spanish arms. 1—R. Good, very rare. 18$\frac{1}{2}$. 1

307 1828–82 $\frac{1}{4}$, $\frac{1}{2}$ (2), 1 and 2 Rls., 5, 10 (2, Max. and Rep.) and 25 Ctvs. Good to fine. 9

308 Guatemala. Ferd. VII, 1816 $\frac{1}{2}$ Real ; '17 1 do. Both unc. 2 do. Good. Rep., 1824 $\frac{1}{2}$, '31 $\frac{1}{4}$ Rls. Good. 5

309 Ferd. VII, 1821 8 Rls. Fine. 1

310 Costa Rica. 1846 2 Rls. Sun and mts. ℞ Tree sep. 2—R.
A necessity coin struck on Guat. cob piece. Holed. The
best I have seen. 19 x 22.   1
311 1849 Rl. Female bust. 1875 25 Ctvs. Both fine. Dominican Rep. 1891 Francs. Unc. Windward Is., 1732 6 Sous.
Very fair.   4
312 New Granada. 1837–54 ½, 1, 2 (2 types) Rls., also Decimo.
Good to fine.   6
313 Ecuador. 1834 Rl, '40 2 do. Sun and mts. '46 2 do. Bust
type. Good.   3
314 Peru. Ferd. VI, 1753 4 Rls. '56 ½ do. Lima mint. Globe
and pillar type. The first has a few Chinese chop marks.
Good.   2
315 1827–66 ¼, ½, 1 (2) and 2 Reals, also ⅕ Sol. 1 fair, others
mostly choice.   6
316 Cuzco. 1837 ¼ Real. Sun in splendor. ℞ Castle within
wrth. Fair, very rare. 16.   1
317 Bolivia. 1737 2 Rls, Potosi, Cob. Fair. 1863 Sldo (2, one
the beehive type). 1865 ½ Blvno. Busts l. 1871 20 Ctvs.
Good.   5
318 Chile. 1834 to '77 Santiago Rl, 1 and 2 do., arms. Condor
flying, and on shld, each ½ and 1 Dcmo. Good to fine, some
brilliant.   7
319 Venezuela. 1874 ¼ Blvno. Caracas. 1818 2 Rls, '29 ¼ do.
cornucopia. Uruguay. 1877 10 Ctmo. Good to fine.   4
320 Brazil. 1837 to '67 100, 200, 500 and 1000 Reis. Arms.
'68 500 do. Bust. All fine.   5
321 La Plata. 1815 ½ Real. Sun in splendor, without mark of
value. Potosi mint. Fine and rare. 16.   1
322 1826 2 Slds. Sim. to last. Rioja mint. 1843 2 Rls. Mt
above cannon crossed. Both fine.   2
323 England. Sceattae. Similar to Hawkins's 42. V. good.   1
324 Aethelred II, 978–1016 Penny. Very good.   1
325 Edward the Confessor. Penny. Bust l., with sceptre.
Fine.   1
326 William I or II, 1066–1100 Penny. Pax type. Very good,
slight dent through face.   1
327 Henry II, 1154–89 Penny. Bust facing, with sceptre. Fair,
scarce.   1

328 Henry III. Pennies of Canterbury, London and Winchester.
Good to fine.   5
329 Edw. II, London Penny. Hy V or VI, London Groat. V. gd.   2
330 Edw. IV, London Groat. Fine. Another, of York. Fair.   2
331 Henry VII, London Groat. Half Groats, Canterbury (Wm.
Wareham) and York. The last two in profile. 2 fair, 1 fine.   3
332 Hy VIII, Tower Groat. Bust in profile. V. good. Edw. VI,
1549 (in Roman numerals) Testoon. Bust r. V. fair.   2
333 Edw. VI, Shil. Poor. Phil. and Mary, 1554 6d. Very fair.
Eliz., 3 Halfp. and Half Groat, both London. Good.   4
334 Eliz., 1562 Milled 6d. m.m. a star. Very good.   1
335 Jas. I, Penny. Chas. I, 1 and 2 do. Good.   3
336 Chas. I, Tower 6d. m.m. anchor. V. fine. Obv. shows slight
planchet filemarks.   1
337 Commonwealth Penny. 1654 6d. V. good.   2
338 Chas. II, 2, 3 and 6d. Milled money, 1675-6. Good and fine.
Also an early Penny of the Crux type, similar to Aethelred,
barbaric work. Good. Etc.   5
339 Chas. II, 4d. 3rd coinage, and 1 and 4d. 4th coinage. Fine.   3
340 Jas. II, 1686 Shil. 1687 1 and 2d. Maundy. All fine.   3
341 Wm. and Mary, 1693 Shil. W and M linked in angles. V.
good. 1694 2d. '96 4d. Fine.   3
342 William III, 1696 6d. and Shil. '98 1d. '99 3d. 1701 2d.
One good, others fine.   5
343 Anne, 1, 2, 3 and 4d. Maundy. Also 6d. and Shil. (the last
E. mint, v. good), others v. fine, a most desirable lot.   5
344 Geo. I, 1, 2, 3 and 4d. Maundy. Fine. S. S. Co. Shil., 1723.
V. fine.   5
345 Geo. II, 1, 2 and 4d. Maundy. Young head. 1760 6d. Old
hd. All v. fine.   4
346 Geo. III, 1762 3d. '72 4d. '82 2 and 3d. '87 Shil. 1800
1d. Shilling fine, others v. fine and choice.   6
347 Token 6d., 1812. Beehive. Shil. by Joseph Hick, Exeter.
18d., 1811, J. B. Monk, Reading. Good to fine.   3
348 Geo. IV, Maundy Set, 1822-30. In very choice condition.   4
349 1824 6d. '25 Lion Shil. Wm. IV, 1834 1½ and 6d. and Shil.
V. good.   5
350 Wm. IV, Maundy Set, 1831-33. V. fine.   4
351 Victoria, 1843 1½d. '54 4d. '66 6d. and Shil. Gd to fine.   4

352 Maundy Set, 1856-59. V. fine. 4
353 Colonial. Canada. 1858-74 5, 10, 20 and 25 Cents. Fine to unc. 4
354 Hong Kong, 5 and 10c. India, 2 Annas, 1822, anchor type $\frac{1}{8}$ and $\frac{1}{4}$ Dols. Good to fine. 5
355 Scotland. Wm. the Lion, 1165-1214. Penny of the 2d coinage. Hd *l.*, with sceptre. Good. 1
356 Alex. III, Penny. Robt. II, Perth Groat. Also Mary I, Billon Bawbee. Good. 3
357 Jas. V, Groat, 3d coinage (1527) with bust *r*. Robertson, type 2. Fine. 1
358 Ireland. John, 1199-1216. Baptist $\frac{1}{2}$d. Good. Hy VIII and Jane Seymour, Groat. Poor. 2
359 John, Dublin Penny. Bust in triangle. V. good. 1
360 Geo. III, 1805 and '13. Bank Tokens for 10d. Gd and fair. 2
361 France. Louis le Debonnaire, 814-40. Denier, Temple type. Good. Chas. VI, 1380-1422. Blanc. V. fine. Chas. VII, 1422-61. Gros, Crown type. Good. 3
362 Louis XI, 1461-83. Blanc. Fine. Francis I, 1514-46. Half Teston. Fair. Hy II, 1560 $\frac{1}{2}$ Teston. Fair. Last two with bust. 3
363 Hy III, 1577 Base Douzaine. 1587 Franc, with bust. Hy IV, 1602 $\frac{1}{4}$ Ecu of Navarre. V. gd, the latter nearly fine. 3
364 Louis XIII, 1642 $\frac{1}{12}$ Ecu. '43 $\frac{1}{4}$ do. Louis XIV, 1644 $\frac{1}{12}$ do. Louis XV, 1749 6 Sols. '56 12 do. '74 24 do. One fair, others good. 6
365 Louis XVI, 1788 $\frac{1}{10}$ and $\frac{1}{5}$ Ecu. '91 15 Sols, Genius type. Fine and v. fine. 3
366 1792 5 Fcs, Bordeaux mint. ℞ Genius ins. tablet. V. gd. 1
367 Nap., First Consul. 1 Franc. Fair. Emperor, $\frac{1}{4}$ and 1 do. with Rep. on *rev*. 1809 2 do. '13 $\frac{1}{2}$ do., with Empire on *rev*. Very good. 5
368 Louis XVIII, 1822 Franc. '24 $\frac{1}{4}$ do. Chas. X, 1827 $\frac{1}{2}$ and 2 do. 1830 1 do. Last two exceptionally fine, others v. gd. 5
369 Louis Phil., 1845 $\frac{1}{4}$ Franc. '46 25 and 50 Ctms. '47 2 Fcs. Rep., 1850 20 Ctms. '51 1 Fc. Fine to unc. 6
370 Aquitaine. Bern. Guil., 984-1010. Denier. Besançon, 1613 Carolu. Dauphine, Carolu. Lorraine, Teston, Leop. J, 1712, with bust. Good. 4

24 FOREIGN SILVER.

371 Melle. Charlemagne, Denier. Poitou. Richard, 1169–96. Denier. Provens. Thibaut II, 1525–52. Denier. Vienna. Deniers of the Archbishops. Good to fine. 5

372 Spain. Peter, 1350–69 Real de Plata. P cwnd. 25. Ferd. and Is., Real. Phil. IV, 1643 2 do. Chas. II, 1689 ½ do. Good to fine. 4

373 Chas. III, Pretender, 1712 2 Reals. Louis I, 1724 (only year of coinage) 2 Reals. Phil. V, 1725, '32 1 do. Jos. Nap., 1813 2 do. Ferd. VII, 1816 Medio. Good. 6

374 Ferd. VII, 1822 10 Rls. Bust within circle of arrow-heads and beads. Fine. 35. 1

375 Isab. II, 1 and 2 Rls and 40c de Esc., different types, 1850 to '67. One good, two fine. 3

376 Rep., 1870 1 and 2 Pesetas. A select pair in mint state. 2

377 Barcelona. Ferd., 1412–16. Groat. Hd l. Fair. 24. Phil. III, 1612. Bust l. V. good. 17. 2

378 Dirhems of the Khalifs (2). Mediaeval Pennies, etc. Four are fine. 6

379 Portugal. Jos. I, 50, 150 Reis. 1763 2 Macutas for African possessions. Peter V, 50 Reis. Good. 4

380 Norway. Oscar II, 10 Sk. Hd. 10 Ore. Arms. Denmark. Fred. III, 2 Sk. Fred. IV, 1705 Schil. for Schleswig-H. 1708 8 Sk. Good to fine. 5

381 Sweden. Chas. XII, 1697 ¹⁄₂₄ R. Daler ,(for Bremen and V.), also 2 Mks with his bust. 29. Gust. III to Os. II, small coins. Mostly good to fine. 7

382 Flanders. Mary of Burgundy, 1477 Dbl Briquet. Gd. 27. 1

383 Flanders, Holland, Netherlands, Tournay (15)83, Utrecht, Zeelandia, Belgium. Size 20 Ctms to ⅓ Ecu. Gd to v. fine. 8

384 Cologne, early Denier. Mayence, Bracteate. Denier, Hy II. Misnie, Groschen. Poor to good. 4

385 Augsburg, Bamburg, Brunswick-L., Carinthia, Lubeck, Munsterburg-O., etc., 17th, 18th and 19th centuries (3 of latter), mostly above 10c. size, including a Swiss Franc. Generally fine. 14

386 Montfort, Munster, Tyrol, etc. About ⅓ Thaler size, 17th, 18th and 19th centuries. 1 good, others fine. 5

387 Italy. Nap. I, 5, 10 Soldi, 1, 2 Lire, 1810–12. Good to fine. 4

388 Vic. Em., 20, 50 Ctmi (2 types), 1 Lira. Lucca. 1806 1 Fc.
Parma. 1815 10 Soldi. 2 good, others fine. 6

389 Bergamo. Fred. II, 1237 Pesaro. G. Ubaldi. Giulio. Fair.
27. Sardinia. Chas. Felix, 1826 50 Ctmi. Vic. Em. II
50 do. (2 var.), 2 Lire. Good. 6

390 Tuscany. Leop. II, 1842 Fiorino. '56 30 Soldi. Venice.
Jo. Grad., 1355–56 Matapane. Lud. Manin, 1790 ¼ Tallero.
Female bust. Greece. Otho, ¼ Dchm. George, 50 Lep.
Malta. F. Ximenes, 4 Tari, bust. Good to fine. 7

391 Papal. Alex. VII, ½, 1 Grosso. Clem. X, Inn. XII, Clem.
XI (3 types), Grossi. Benedict XIV, Sede Vacante, 1758
Grossi. Mostly v. good. 9

392 Clem. XII, Giulio. Clem. XIII, Pius VI, 2 do. and 5 Bai (for
Bologna). Pius IX, 5, 10 Bai. 1 fair, others good to fine. 6

393 Naples and Sicily. Phil. II, ½ Carlino. Poor. Charles II,
1684 Testone. '96 20 Grossi. Ferd. II, 10, 20 Grani.
Good to v. fine. 5

394 Russia. Eliz., 1753 Griv., with bust. Good. Nich. I, 5, 20
Kopecks. Finland. 1868 25 Pen. Fine. 4

395 Lithuania. Sig. Aug., 1568 4 Grosch. Bust. Fair. Livonia.
Eliz., 1757 4 Kop. Arms. Riga. Sig. III, 1596 3 Grosch.
Bust. Good. 3

396 Turkey, 3 and 5c. size. Tunis, 3 and 50c. size. Present century. 3 are fine. 4

397 India. ½, 1 Rupee (native work), and 1, 2 Annas, ¼, ½, 1 Rupee, about 1835, from Calcutta and other mints. Mostly
fine. 7

398 Madras. Chas. II, Dbl Fanam. 2 Cs linked. Ned. Ind.; $\frac{1}{10}$,
¼ Guld. Siam. ⅛ Tical. Elephant and pagodas. Good
to fine. 4

399 Japan. Bean shape, 15 x 19, also Bu and round coins of 5, 10,
20 Sen, without English value. Good to fine. 5

BRONZE MEDALS.

400 Canada. 1829. Bust Wm. I, Netherlands. Arbitration on
limits bet. Canada and U. S. LeR. 830. V. fine. 42. 1

401 U. S. Franklin. Inst. Penn. Award. 38. Hosack, M. D.
32. Both fine. Lafayette, the Defender, etc. 46. Good. 3

402 Centl., 1881, Battle of Groton Heights, Massacre in Fort Gris-
     wold and burning of New London. V. fine. 39½.   1
403 Lovett's series, 2. Sage's. 4. Boston Num. Soc. Maj. Genl.
     Hooker. All v. fine. 31.   8
404 England. Marq. of Anglesey, 1815, by *Mills*. Lord Exmouth,
     Mudie series. John Moore, by *Peter Wyon*. Fine, some
     corrosion on *revs*. All 40.   3
405 Sir Wm. P. Carroll, 1809. 40. Rich'd Cobden, Champion of
     Free Trade, 1846. 38. Lord North, by *Kirk*. 36. Very
     fine.   3
406 Alfred, 1849. Jubilee, 1000 years. 35. Stephen, by *Dassier*.
     40. Edw. VI, Religious Declaration. 51. Webster's Nu-
     mismatic Medal, with coinages from Wm. I to Vic. 44. The
     last 2 in w.m. Fine.   4
407 Series Numismatica. Ariosto, Boerhaave (Physician), Cano-
     va. Fine. 41.   3
408 Others. Cimarosa, Congreve, Gessner, Handel. Fine. 41.   4
409 Others. Samuel Johnson (dents on *rev*.), La Caille, Lavater.
     Fine. 41.   3
410 Others. Milton (Poet, 2 vars.), Moreau, Sanvedra. Fine. 41.   4
411 France. Louis XIV, 1662. ℞ Justice stdg. 1666, Alliance
     with Holland. M. I., Vol. I, 159, both by *Mauger*. Fine. 41.   2
412 Nap. I, 1796. Battle of Montenotte. 40. 1799, Landing at
     Alex. 39. 1840, Arrival of his remains at Paris. 25. All
     with bust. Fine.   3
413 1809. Porte St. Martin and Carinthie. Treaty of Pressburg.
     Fine. 40.   2
414 1815. Duke D'Angouleme. 40. 1817. Prince de Conde
     (good). 41. Hy IV and Louis XVIII, busts conjoined. 32.
     Fine.   3
415 Louis XVIII. Good. 40. Also his bust with Louis XIV.
     25. Count de Chambord. 36½. Balbi, Venetian geog-
     rapher. 41. Fine.   4
416 Galerie Metallique. Destouches, La Fontaine, Mirabeau.
     Fine. 41.   3
417 Illustrious Men. Rousseau, Saussure (Physicist). Fine. 40.   2
418 Incomplete set of French Kings. From Pharamond, No. 1,
     A. D. 417, to No. 68, Louis XVII, 1793. All with busts.
     ℞ Date of birth, reign and death. V. fine. 32.   48

419 Medalets with die-projecting loop. Thiers, McMahon, Gam-
betta, Prince Imp., etc. V. fine. Brass.   16
420 Papal. A. D. 79 to 1522. Anacletus. 37. Anterus. 37.
Julian II. 41. Leo X. 32. Adrian VI. 41. V. fine.   5
421 1525-55. Clem. VII. 34. Paul III. 41 and 34. Julius
III. 33. Marcellus II. 31. Fine.   5
422 1555-72. Paul IV. Pius IV and V. Greg. XIII, Massacre
of St. Bartholomew. All fine. 30.   4
423 1572-92. Greg. XIII. 37. Sixtus V. 34. Greg. XIV. 34.
Inn. IX. 34. Clem. VIII. 33. Fine.   5
424 1605-55. Paul V. 38. Urban VIII. 40. Alex. VII. 41.
1 good, 2 fine.   3
425 1655-91. Alex. VII. 39. Clem. X. 35. Inn. XI. 36, 38.
Inn. XII. 30. Fine.   5
426 1700-30. Clem. XI. 37 (2 subjects). Inn. XIII. 33. Ben.
XIII. 33. Clem. XII. 33. 1 good, others fine.   5
427 1740-1800. Ben. XIV. 36. Clem. XIII and XIV. 34.
Pius VI. 34. Pius VII. 36. Fine.   5
428 1800-46. Pius VII. 41. Leo XII. 41. Sede Vacante. 31,
36. Pius IX. 43. Fine.   5

SILVER MEDALETS, ETC.

429 Washington, Nap. I, Louis XVIII, etc. Fine. 12½ to 18.   4
430 England, Chas. II, Coronation. Louisa of Denmark. Henry
IV, France. Jewish Token, Shekel design, etc. 1 fair,
others fine. 17 to 30.   6
431 Spanish Procl. Pieces. Half Reales, 1789, Madrid and Mahon.
Reales, 1808, Guatemala (2 var.), Madrid, San Salvador.
1823, Seville. Good to fine, a choice and rare lot.   7

BOOKS, CATALOGUES, ETC.

432 De Bye, J. Imperatorvm Romanorvm Nvmismata Avrea.
247 pp., 64 plates. 4to, full vellum. In fine condition.
Antwerp, 1727.   1
433 Rubenii, A. Regum et Imperatorum Romanorum Numisma-
tum. 115 pp., 68 plates. Folio, boards. In fine condition.
Brandenburg, 1700.   1

28   ANCIENTS.

434 Ursini. Familiae Romanae qvae reperivntvr in Antiqvis nv-
    mismatibvs. 403 pp., plates inserted in text. Folio, full
    vellum. Fine condition. Rome, 1577. One of the earliest
    compilations on Numismatics.   1

435 Unpriced Catalogues of American Sales, 1876, '77 (2), '78 (3),
    '79 (17), '80 (4), '81 (5), '82 (15), '83 (3), '84 (4), '85 (10),
    '86 (6), '87 (4), '89, '92 (3). Free from duplicates.   78

*THE COLLECTION OF THOMAS H. SHEPPARD, OF
PITTSBURGH, PA.*

ANCIENTS.

436 Greek Copper. Carthago Nova, Bruttium, Brundisium, Com-
    pulteria, Neapolis, etc., named in envelopes. Many good.   17
437 Imperial times. Augustus, Tiberius, etc. His. Citerior, Julia
    Traducta, Romula, Cascantum, Celsa, etc. S. B. to G. B.
    Fair to v. good.   10
438 Greek Silver. Tarentum, B. C. 400–360. Didr. Syracuse,
    B. C. 480–415. Tetr. Abdera, B. C. 430–408. Didr.
    Apollonia. Dchm. Poor to v. fair.   4
439 Macedonia under the Romans, B. C. 158–146. Artemis, hd
    on Macedonian shld. Tetr. V. fair. Thasos, after B. C.
    146. Hd of young Dionysus *r*. Tetr. Cut in centre of
    rev., otherwise good.   2
440 Apollonia, B. C. 229–100. Victoriatus and its half, B. C.
    100–27. Denarius, Apollo hd *l.* Dyrrachium, B. C. 229–100
    Victoriatus. Fair to good.   4
441 Anactorium, abt B. C. 350. Didr. Good. Boeotia, B. C.
    379–338. Stater. Good, deep saw-cut from edge. Thes-
    piae, B. C. 387–374. Obol. Poor.   3
442 Macedonia. Alex. III. Good. Parthia. Fair. Drachms.   2
443 Galatia. Amyntas, B. C. 36–25. Pallas head *r*. ℞ AMYN-
    TOY, etc. Nike advancing *l.* Tetr. Fine.   1
444 Syria. Demetrius I, B. C. 162–151. King's hd *r*. ℞ Tyche
    enthroned. *Obv.* fair, *rev.* good. Tetr.   1
445 Roman consular Denarii. Afrania, Antonia (2 types), Julia,
    Marcia, Salvia. Good to fine.   6

446 Roman Imperial Small Bronze. Claudius I, Gallienus to Arcadius, 14 reigns. A few duplicate types, mostly v. good.   24
447 Second Bronze. Claud. I (2 types of *rev.*), Nero, Faust. I
(2 types). All fine.   5
448 Claud. I (2), Nero (2), Ant. Pius, Faust. I (3), Sev. Alex. (3),
Maximus. Mostly v. good.   12
449 Faust. I, Sev. Alex., Julia Mamaea, Maximinus I. 2 types of
each. Good to fine.   8
450 Faust. I (2), Sev. Alex., Julia Mamaea (2), Gratianus, Theod.
Honorius, Arcadius (2). Poor to good.   11
451 Silver Denarii. M. Antony and Augustus. Their hds, each in
profile *r.* Good, rare.   1
452 Lucilla (fair), M. Aurel., Faust. II, Julia Domna, Caracalla,
Plautilla, Elagabalus, Phil. I. Fine.   8
453 M. Aurel. (2, 1 plated), Faust. II, Julia Domna, Caracalla (3),
Elagabalus. Good to fine.   8
454 Byzantine Silver. Justinus I, Theodoricus and Just. I (holed),
Anastasius and Theod. Fine. 11 to 13.   3
455 Constantinus X, 911–59, Johannes I, 969–75, do. II, 1118–43.
Fine. 20 to 22. Rare.   3

UNITED STATES.

456 **Colonial, etc.** Wood ½d. 1723. Vermont (3), Mass., New
Jersey (5), Virginia, Fugio. Poor to v. good ; of the latter 5.   12
457 Connecticut. 1785, '86, '87, '88. Hds *r* and *l.* Varieties.
Poor to v. good ; fewest of last.   18
458 Duplicates. Conn. (3), Va. (6), Fugio. Poor to good.   10
459 1652 Mass. Pine-tree Shilling, small planchet, rather poor.   1
460 1652 Another. Large planchet, die broken through date,
parts of legend weak ; otherwise v. good.   1
461 1783 Chalmers Annapolis Shilling. Good, not well centred.   1
462 1792 Half Disme. Fair ; 2 dents on *obv.*   1
463 Hard Times tokens, Merchants' cards and War cards (at least
4 of Pittsburgh and vicinity). Good.   38
464 Confederate States. Impression from *obv.* die after cancella-
tion by J. W. Scott. Another with the *rev.* "4 originals,"
etc. ; the opposite side has incused *obv.* of the U. S. ½
Dol. of 1861. Brass. Both fine and *unique.*   2

465 Paper Money. Colonial. New Jersey (2), Delaware, Penn. (4, including 15 and 20 sh. 1758), Maryland (12). Only 1 duplicate. Mostly good.

466 Fractional Currency. 1st issue, 5, 10, 25c.; 2nd, 5, 10, 25, 50c.; 3rd, 3, 10, 25, 50c.; 4th, 10, 15c.; 5th, 50c.; 2nd series of 5th, 10, 25, 50c. Mostly good to new and crisp. Face value $3.78.

467 Others poor to fine. Face value $5.20.

468 **Half Cents.** 1793, v. poor; '94, '95, plain and lettered edge; '97, fair.

469 1795 Lettered edge, v. fair; '97, 1800, good.

470 1802 Very fair, rare.

471 1803, '04 (2 var.) to '11. Fair to good (1 poor).

472 1804 (3), '05, '06, '08, '09 (2), '28, '35 (2), '49, '51, etc. Poor to v. good.

473 1825, '26, '28, '29, '32 to '35, '49, '51, '53 to '57. Mostly good to fine.

474 **Cents.** 1793 Chain, AMERICA. About good, very dark.

475 1793 Liberty cap. Rather poor, date good.

476 1794 (2 var.), '95. Plain and lettered edge. Barely fair and fair.

477 1795 Plain edge. '96 Lib. cap. Good.

478 1796 Lib. cap and bust. '97, '98, 1800 (over 17). V. fair.

479 1796 LIHERTY. Nearly good; seldom found above poor.

480 1797, '98, 1800 (2 var.), '01, '02 (no stems), '03. V. fair.

481 1801 HNITED and $\frac{1}{000}$, '02 $\frac{1}{000}$. V. fair to good.

482 1802 Stems and no stems. '03 Small and large $\frac{1}{100}$. Fair to nearly fine.

483 1805 V. good. '06 V. fair.

484 1807 over '06, Perfect date, small and large $\frac{1}{100}$, '08, '10 over '09, and perfect date. Fair to v. good.

485 1811 over '10. V. fair. Perfect date. V. good, although a bad scratch extends from edge to nose.

486 1812 Small and large date. '13, '14 Plain and crosslet 4. Fair to v. good.

487 1816, '17 (3 vars., 1 with 15 stars), '18 (2 dups., v. choice), '19 small and large date, and over '18. Good to fine.

488 1820 over 19 and perfect date, '21, '22, '24, '25. V. fair to v. good.

489	1821, '23 over '22, '24, v. fair ; '26, nearly fine ; '27, good.	5
490	1823 Perfect date, v. good.	1
491	1828 Sm. and lge date, '29, '30, '31. Good and v. good.	8
492	1834, '35, old and new head ; '36 to '39, booby ; '40, sm. date. Good and v. good.	8
493	1839 over '36. V. fair, rare.	1
494	1841, '42, lge date ; '43 to '48. Good to nearly fine.	8
495	1848 to '57, with dups. of '55 and '56. Good to unc.	11
496	**Small Cents.** 1856. Flying eagle. Good, very rare.	1
497	1857 to '89. Lacking '59, '82, '83. Unc. and proof ; most of former.	30
498	**Two Cents.** 1864 to '71. Unc., red.	7
499	1873 Proof. Rarest of series.	1
500	**Three Cents, Nickel.** 1865 to '74. Good.	10
501	1875 to '89 (excepting '77). The '87 is over '86. Unc. 2, remainder proof.	14
502	1877 Proof. Rarest of series.	1
503	**Five Cents, Nickel.** 1867 to '71, '79, '80, '81, '84 to '89. Unc. and proof.	14
504	1877 Proof. Rare.	1
505	**Trimes.** 1851 (O. and P. mints) to '73. Set complete. The '65 and '70 good, remainder mostly unc. or proof.	24
506	Others, 1851 to '62, 3 of each date. Mostly fine, a few unc.	36
507	1851 to '62, 4 of each date. Mostly fine.	48
508	1851 to '62 ; 1 of '55 ; other dates well assorted. Mostly good, some fine.	50
509	**Half Dimes.** 1795, good, scratched ; 1800, poor, date good ; '01, v. poor, with large hole.	3
510	1829 to '37, v. fine to uncirculated.	9
511	1829 to '33, 3 each ; '34 to '37, 2 each. Very fine, mostly choice.	23
512	1829 (2), '30 (3), '31 (4), '32 (8), '35 (5). As last.	22
513	1837 Starless ; '38, '39, O. and P. ; '40, with and without drapery ; '41, '42, O. mint ; '43, '44, '45, '47, '48, '49. V. fine, many choice.	14
514	1837 Starless (4), '38 (4), '39 (2), '40 (2), '41 (3), '43 (4), '44 (4). Mostly v. fine.	23
515	1837 Starless (4), '38 (4), '43 (3), '44 (4), '45 (6), '47 (4). As last.	25

516 1837 Starless (3), '38 (4), '45 (6), '48 (2), '49 (5). Mostly
fine.   20
517 1843 Sharp, unc. A few faint scratches, noticeable only
under a glass.   1
518 1846 Very fair. Rare.   1
519 1850 to '56. Each O. and P. excepting '52 and '53, arrowless.
Good to fine, chiefly of latter.   14
520 1850 (3), '51, '52 (4), '53 arrows (6), '54 (3), '55 (2), '56 (4).
As last.   23
521 1854 (3), '56 (3), '57 (3), '58, '60. The last O. mint unc. (8) ;
others good to fine and sharp.   20
522 1857, '58, both dates O. and P. ; '59, O. ; '60, O. and P. ; '61,
'62, '63 (S.) Good to unc.   10
523 1857 (4), '58 (5), '60, '60, O. mint (unc. 8), '61, '62 (2). V.
good.   21
524 1860 O. mint. Uncirculated.   12
525 1860 Another lot as last.   12
526 1860 Another.   18
527 1860 Another.   18
528 1863 V. fine, sharp. About unc.   1
529 1864, '65 (S. mint). V. good.   2
530 1866 to '69. Ex. fine to unc.   4
531 1869 S. mint, fair ; '70 to '73, good to fine.   5
532 **Dimes.** 1796. Very fine, seldom equalled, slight cut on *rev.*
edge ; rare.   1
533 1797. 6 stars facing. Fine, an uncommon condition, slight
scratch from Y to nose ; rare.   1
534 1798 over '97. V. fair, rare.   1
535 1800, '05, '06. Poor, dates v. plain.   3
536 1801 Good, scratched on face and before nose.   1
537 1805, '07, '09, poor, dates plain ; '11, good, plugged.   4
538 1811 Very good.   1
539 1814 Large date, nearly fine.   1
540 1814 Sm. date ; '20, '21, sm. and lge date ; '23, poor and fair. 5
541 1821 Lge date ; '23, '24, '27. Fair to v. good.   5
542 1822 Fair, edge cut. Rare.   1
543 1822, '24, '27 (4). Poor and fair, dates plain.   6
544 1828 Sm. and lge date ; '29 to '32. Mostly good.   6
545 1828 (sm. date) to '35, with dups. of '33 and '34. As last.   10

546	1832, '34, '35. V. fine, 2 brilliant.	3
547	1836, '37, with and without stars ; '38, O. and P. mints ; '39, O. and P. ; '40, '41, O. mint ; '42. Fair to v. good.	10
548	1837 Bust, '42, '43, O. and P. ; '44, '45, O. and P. ; '47, '48, '49. Mostly good.	10
549	1837 Extra fine ; '38, O. mint, unc. Both without stars.	2
550	1840 With drapery. V. good, scarce.	1
551	1846 Good, scarce.	1
552	1846, '50, '51, O. mint ; '52, '53, arrows ; '54, '56, sm. and lge date ; '57, O. and P. Fair to v. good.	10
553	1858, '59, '60, P. and S. ; '61, '68 (poor), '69. Last 2 S. mint. Fair and good.	7
554	1863, '64. Proofs, both scarce.	2
555	1865, '67. Proofs, the first tarnished, the latter slightly blemished ; '71, '72, '73 (2 var.), '74, '75, '76 (C. C. mint). Poor and fair.	9
556	1878 to '89. 3 proofs, 4 unc., others good to fine.	13
557	**Twenty Cents.** 1875, S. mint, '76. Fine.	2
558	1877 Proof. A few haymarks. Rare.	1
559	1878 Proof. Shows slight marks of brushing. Rare.	1
560	1878 Proof. Slight tarnish ; spot at Lib. cap.	1
561	**Quarter Dols.** 1796 V. fair, holed. 1804 Poor. Date strong.	2
562	1805, '06, '07. V. fair and good.	3
563	1805, '06 (3), '07. Poor to good.	5
564	1815, '18, '19. Fair to good.	3
565	1815, '18, '19, '21. Fair to good.	4
566	1820, '21 (v. good, nearly fine), '22. Good.	3
567	1822, '25, '28 (2). V. fair.	4
568	1824 V. fair, scarce.	1
569	1825 V. good. '28 Nearly good. Both scratched lightly on obv.	2
570	1831 Fine. '35 V. fine, a trifle less than unc.	2
571	1831, '32 Good. '33 Poor.	3
572	1834, '35, '36 Good.	3
573	1837, '38 Bust. '38 Liberty std. V. good, nearly fine.	3
574	1839 Fine and sharp.	1
575	1893 Isabella Columbian. Unc., brill.	1
576	1893 Isabella. Unc.	1

577	1893 Three more. As last.	3
578	1893 Others. As last.	5
579	**Half Dols.** 1794 Very good, rare.	1
580	1795 Three leaves below wings. V. good.	1
581	1795 Vars. and differing from last. Good.	2
582	1795 Others. V. fair.	2
583	1795 Others. One poor, two fair.	3
584	1801 Good, rare.	1
585	1802 Very good, rare.	1
586	1803 Large 3. V. good, nearly fine.	1
587	1803, '05 Very good.	2
588	1803 About good.	3
589	1805 over '04. Very fair, scarce.	1
590	1805 Perfect date. '06 Without stem to branch. V. good, nearly fine.	2
591	1805 (2), '06. Ptd 6, without stem. Good to nearly fine.	3
592	1806 over 6 inverted. V. good. Scratched through field and face. Scarce.	1
593	1806 Ptd and knob'd 6. V. good, nearly fine.	2
594	1806 Ptd and knob'd. '07 Good.	3
595	1806 Ptd (2) and knob'd. '07 Good.	4
596	1807 Bust *r.* and *l.*, the latter 50c. over 20. V. good.	2
597	1807 Bust *r.* and *l.*, 3 each. Good and v. good.	6
598	1808 over '07 and perfect date. '09 V. good.	3
599	1808, '09, 2 each. Good and v. good.	4
600	1810, '11. Fine. A trifle less than unc.	2
601	1810 Nearly fine. '11 Small and large date. Fair and good.	3
602	1810, '11, 2 each. Good and v. good.	4
603	1812 over '11, also perfect date. '13 Good and v. good.	3
604	1812, '13. Others, precisely as last.	3
605	1814 Vars. of *rev.* '17 Good to fine.	3
606	1814, '17, 2 each. Good.	4
607	1815 Very good, rare.	1
608	1817 Punctuated date. About fine.	1
609	1818 over '17. Nearly fine. Perfect date. V. fine.	2
610	1818, '19, 2 each. Good to fine.	4
611	1819 over '18 V. fine. '19 Perfect date. V. good. '20 over '19 Fine.	3
612	1820 Close, perfect date. Fine. '21 Nearly fine.	2

613	1820, '21 (2). V. good.	3
614	1821, '22 (2). Good.	3
615	1823, '24 over '21, also perfect date. Good to v. fine.	3
616	1823, '24. Both with vars. in date.	4
617	1824 Perfect date, '25, '26. V. good to fine.	3
618	1825, '26, '27. Fine.	3
619	1826, vars. in date, '27. V. good to nearly fine.	3
620	1826 (2), '27. About fine.	3
621	1828 Straight base 2. Ex. fine, brill. Curled base 2 V. gd. '29 Fine.	3
622	1828, '29 (2), '30. About fine.	4
623	1830 Small and large o in date. V. fine, the first about unc. '31 Fine.	3
624	1830, '31, '32. Fine.	3
625	1832 Large letters in legend. V. fine, brill., scarce.	1
626	1832 (2), '33, '34. About fine.	4
627	1833, '34. Large date, small and large letters on *rev*. V. fine.	3
628	1834 Small date, '35, '36. Fine to v. fine, bril.	3
629	1835, '36, '37. V. good to about fine.	3
630	1836 Milled edge. V. good, nick on *rev*., scarce.	1
631	1836 Another as last. Good.	1
632	1836 Another quite like the last.	1
633	1837, '38, '39. All bust type. Fine.	3
634	1837, '38, '39. As last, but slightly inferior.	3
635	1839 Lib. std. Fine, brill., light nicks. '41, '42. Good, the latter O. mint.	3
636	1841 O. mint, '46, '61. Good to fine.	3
637	1852 O. mint. V. fair, rare.	1
638	1892, '93. Columbian ; the first in fine leather case. Unc.	2
639	1892 Columbian. Unc., some light nicks.	4
640	1892, '93. Columbian (3 each). V. fine to unc.	6
641	1893 Columbian. Unc., light nicks.	6
642	A collection of Half Dols., every date issued between 1801 and 1836 ; includes a very fair 1815 and a good milled edge '36. Many good.	37

SECOND DAY'S SALE.

UNITED STATES SILVER.

643 **Dollars.** 1795 Hd. 3 leaves below wings. Good.
644 1795 Hd, 2 and 3 leaves below wings. Fair.
645 1795 Bust. Very good, nearly fine.
646 1795 Another, from same dies as last. Good.
647 1795 Another. Good.
648 1796 Small date. Fair, scratched at nose.
649 1799 Large date. Very good.
650 1797 Seven stars facing. Good.
651 1797 As last. About good.
652 1797 Another, not quite equal to last.
653 1798 13 stars, small eagle *rev.* V. good, nearly fine, rare.
654 1798 15 stars facing, with small eagle *rev.* About as last, nick before face, and another in centre of *rev.*, rare.
655 1798 Large eagle. Fine, edge defects.
656 1798 Another nearly equal to last.
657 1798 Good, 1 has bad defect on *rev.* edge.
658 1799 Five stars facing. Fair, rare.
659 1799 over '98. V. fair.
660 1799 V. good, cross cut on face.
661 1799 Good.
662 1800 Very fair.
663 1800 Fair. '01 Good, but defect back of head.
664 1801 Nearly good, small cut at R in LIBERTY.
665 1802 over '01. V. good.
666 1802 Perfect date. Good.
667 1802 Many small nicks on *obv.* '03 Similar condition, otherwise both nearly good.
668 1803 Large 3. Fine.

669	1803 A trifle inferior to last.	1
670	1836 Gobrecht on base. Two names scratched in *obv.* field, otherwise good.	1
671	1840 Very good.	1
672	1841 V. fine, a few light nicks.	1
673	1842 Extra fine, a few light nicks and scratches, some mint lustre.	1
674	1843 Fine, a few light nicks.	1
675	1844 Fine, but not quite the equal of last.	1
676	1845 Fine, with light nicks, and *obv.* edge dents.	1
677	1846 Some light nicks and *rev.* edge dents. V. fine.	1
678	1846 V. good, nearly fine.	1
679	1847 Good. '49 V. fair, cross cut in *obv.* field.	2
680	1850 O. mint. Good, scarce.	1
681	1853 Only the slightest marks of circulation ; a beautiful and strong impression, every star filled.	1
682	1856 V. fine, a few light nicks.	1
683	1859 O. and S. mints, '60 O. mint. V. fair, all scarce.	3
684	1860 Very fine.	1
685	1862 Proof, a few light haymarks.	1
686	1862 V. fine and sharp, some slight nicks.	1
687	1863 Fine, many light nicks.	1
688	1864 Proof, very slight blemishes.	1
689	1865 Nearly fine.	1
690	1866 Proof, slight blemishes.	1
691	1867 Condition as last.	1
692	1868 Proof, a few haymarks.	1
693	1869 V. good. '70 V. fine.	2
694	1869 Proof, a trifle less than perfect.	1
695	1869 Fine.	1
696	1871 Proof, a trifle less than perfect.	1
697	1873 Proof, about as last.	1
698	**Trade Dols.** 1873 V. fine, only the slightest marks of circulation.	1
699	1874 Proof, some tarnish.	1
700	1874 S. mint. Fine, many light nicks.	1
701	1875 Proof, slight tarnish.	1
702	1875 Another, quite like the preceding.	1
703	1876 Unc., some mint lustre.	1

704 1877 S. mint. Extremely fine.   1
705 1878 Proof, about perfect.   1
706 1878 Proofs, very slight blemishes.   2
707 1878 Proof, with nicks and scratches. Also S. mint. Fine.   2
708 1879 Proof, with slight nicks and scratches.   1
709 1880 Proof, a few nicks.   1
710 1881 Proof, a few slight scratches.   1
711 1882 Proof, a little better than the preceding.   1
712 1883 Proof, a few slight *obv.* blemishes.   1

PROOF SETS AND PATTERNS.

713 **Minor Proof Sets.** 1879 to '90. The '83 contains three
        5c. pcs.   12
714 1879, 1, 3 and 5 Cents. 25 sets.   25
715 1879 Another lot of 25 sets.   25
716 1880, 1, 3 and 5 Cents. 21 sets.   21
717 1881 (1), '82 (7). Values as last. 8 sets.   8
718 1883 Values as last (2), with three 5c. pcs. (1). 3 sets.   3
719 1884, 1, 3 and 5 Cents. 6 sets.   6
720 1885, 1, 3 and 5 Cents. 13 sets.   13
721 1886, 1, 3 and 5 Cents. 28 sets.   28
722 1886 Another lot of 30 sets.   30
723 1887, 1, 3 and 5 Cents. 7 sets.   7
724 1888, 1, 3 and 5 Cents. 14 sets.   14
725 1889, 1, 3 and 5 Cents. 6 sets.   6
726 1889 Another lot of 25 sets.   25
727 1889 Another lot of 25 sets.   25
728 1889 Another lot of 64 sets.   64
729 1890, 1 and 5 Cents. 3 sets.   3
730 **Full Proof Sets.** 1883, 1, 3, 5 (3), 10, 25, 50c. Trade and
        standard Dols. Slight defects.   1
731 1884, 1, 3, 5, 10, 25, 50c. and Dollar. About perfect.   1
732 1885, 1, 3, 5, 10, 25, 50c. and Dollar. A few defects.   1
733 1885 Another set. As last.   1
734 1886, 1, 3, 5, 10, 25, 50 Cents and Dollar. The 25c. has 1.
        scratched on *obv.* Otherwise as last.   1
735 1887, 1, 3, 5, 10, 25, 50c. and Dollar. Slight tarnish.   1
736 1888, 1, 3, 5 (not proof), 10, 25, 50c. and Dollar. Slight de-
        fects.   1

737 1889, 1, 3, 5, 10, 25, 50c. and Dollar. 50c. has faint scratches
   in field.   1
738 1890, 1, 5, 10, 25, 50c. and Dollar. The 25c. has pin-point
   dent, otherwise the set is brilliant.   1
739 **Patterns.** 1852 Ring Dollar in copper. Unc.   1
740 1854 Cent. Liberty head, no stars. Fine.   1
741 1854 Cent. As last. Fine, slight scratch before chin.   1
742 1854 Cent. Flying eagle. Proof, slight blemishes.   1
743 1855 Cent. Sim. type, large wreath on *rev.* V. fine.   1
744 1856 Half Cent. Regular issue struck in copper nickel.
   About unc.   1
745 1859 Cent. Indian hd *r.* Type of '60. V. fine. 1863 Regular issue. Copper proof.   2
746 1861 Clark, Gruber & Co. $20 in copper. Pike's Peak on
   coronet. V. fine, partly bright.   1
747 1868, 5 Cents. ℞ Large V on garnished shld. Nickel. $10.
   ℞ Sm. spread eagle. Aluminum, milled edge. Proofs.   2
748 1870 Dollar. Indian princess seated on globe. ℞ Value in
   wrth. "Standard" above. Plain edge, copper proof.   1
748a 1879 Dollar. *Barber's obv.* ℞ 898.5s. | 4.2–G. | etc., in dotted
   circle within wrth. V. fine.   1

FOREIGN COPPER COINS.

749 Canada in gen'l and Provinces. Farthing to Penny size. Fair
   to unc. Mostly good.   70
750 Duplicates of last. 1 Far. Remainder Halfp. size. Mostly
   good.   72
751 Mexico. Ferd. VII, 1814, to Rep. 1893. $\frac{1}{16}$, $\frac{1}{8}$, $\frac{1}{4}$ and $\frac{2}{4}$ Rls.
   and Ctvs. Includes the pattern Ctvo. of 1863 in lead, from
   Fischer collection. Mostly v. good.   26
752 British Hond., Nicaragua (nickel), Bermuda, Bahamas, Barbadoes, Antigua, etc., among which, Dan. W. I. 1 Skil.,
   1740, monogram, and 24 do. 1764 Ship. A few poor, mostly
   v. good.   23
753 So. America. Includes Surinam and the Paraguay set, 1870.
   Several large. Mostly good to fine.   38
754 England. Chas. II to Victoria, chiefly of last. $\frac{1}{2}$ Farthing to
   Twopence. Some poor, but mostly fair and good.   71
755 Geo. III, 1797, Twopence. Nearly fine, nick on face.   1

756 Scotland, 1677, Ireland (3), Guernesey (8), Jersey (2). Good
   to unc., red.   14
757 France. Louis XV to present Rep., including a few Baronial
   and Colonial. Poor to fine, some unc.   46
758 Spain. Ferd. VII to Rep. 1870 (6). Portugal, John V to
   Chas. I, 1892, includes 2 unc. sets (21), Gibraltar (2). Poor
   to good.   29
759 Sweden. Christine, 1640, 1 Ore. Arms in shld. ℞ Arrows.
   V. good. 47.   1
760 1715–19 Set of Baron de Gortz Dalers. Hope, Mars, Saturn,
   etc. Fair to v. good.   10
761 Sweden, Norway, Denmark, Low Countries, German States,
   Austria, etc. Includes some unc. sets. Fair to unc.   85
762 Sweden. Plate money, Fred. I. Half Daler, 1750, $4\frac{1}{8}$ x $4\frac{1}{8}$
   inches. Fine.   1
763 Two Dalers, 1733, $6\frac{7}{8}$ x $6\frac{7}{8}$ inches. Fine, but has the appearance of having passed through fire.   1
764 Four Dalers, 1739. V. fair, appearance as last, $9\frac{1}{2}$ x $9\frac{7}{8}$ inches.   1
765 Heinrichstadt. A large square token. Fine, 51 x 54.   1
766 Italy. Varieties in dates and m. m. of Vic. Em., Papal, Roman Rep., Tuscany, Sicily (early), Ionian Is., Corsica,
   Greece, etc. Good to fine.   39
767 Russia, 1728. Moscow Kopeck, 1762. 10 Kop. Cannon,
   flags, etc., and others to 1884. Fair to fine, mostly good.   11
768 Siberia. Cath. II. 10 Kopecks. Sables sup. arms. Fine.
   45. Crimea. 1191=1777. 5 Kopecks. Very good. 45.
   Both rare.   2
769 Turkey, Congo, Egypt, Mombasa, Madeira, Mauritius, etc.
   Good to bright red.   20
770 India (native and British), Siam (including porcelain and lead),
   Ceylon, Sarawak, No. Borneo, China, Japan, Sandwich Is.,
   etc. Good to unc.   62
771 China. Pu (fork-shape coin), struck before the Christian era.
   Good, rare. Length, 48 mlm.   1
772 Hien-Fêng, 1850–61. 50 Cash. Pao-Yuwan. Fine. 44.   1
773 Another as last, for 100 Cash. Pao-Su. Fine. 60.   1
774 Loo-choo Islands. $\frac{1}{2}$ Sjn. Good. 43.   1
775 Foreign Tokens. Mostly English, and chiefly Penny size ; includes an early undated Token of Antwerp (?) Fair to fine.   23

776 Duplicates of many of the preceding lots, with an excess of the present coinage of England, Germany and Austria. Contains some good and uncommon pieces. 263

777 The poor and pierced. The assortment is very general and includes a few Ancient and American Colonial. 274

778 Jetons, Medalets, Spielmarks, Counters, etc., 16th, 17th, 18th and 19th centuries. Chiefly good to fine. 48

779 **Base Coins.** W. I. Isl., etc. (6), European (41), Duplicates (10), also 76 small early bracteates, among which are many similar types. Poor to fine. 133

780 **Nickel Coins.** Mexico (3), Danish W. I. (8), Jamaica (2), U. S. Col. (4), Brazil (2), Roumania (4), etc. Mostly fine to unc. A choice collection. 33

781 Duplicates of last lot, 10 vars. Good to unc. 21

SMALL SILVER.

782 Newfoundland. 1865, 10, 20c. '70, 50c. Good. 3
783 1873, '74, 50c. Good. 2
784 1881, 50c. 1882, 5c. Good. New Brunswick. 1864, 20c. Fine and sharp. 3
785 Colonial. 1822, $\frac{1}{16}$ and $\frac{1}{4}$ Dol. Anchor type. Nearly fine. 2
786 Mexico. Chas. and Joanna, Phil. II, Phil. III, Monogram type. Reals. Fair. 3
787 Phil. V, 1740 $\frac{1}{2}$ and 2 Reals. Chas. III, 1772 $\frac{1}{2}$ do. 1789 Procl. $\frac{1}{2}$ do. Chas. IV, 1808 Real. Last two unc., brill., others good. 5
788 5 and 10 Ctvs, 1 and 2 Rls, 1847-67. Good to v. fine. 5
789 Maximilian, 1866, 10, 50c. Rep., 1885, 25c., also 5 and 10c. present coinage. Good to unc. 5
790 5c. (2), 10c. (2), 25c., 1877-86. Good to unc. 5
791 2 vars. of the Mexican eagle C.S. on 1 Rl pcs. 1 circular, the other in oval depression. Good, rare. 2
792 Guatemala. Chas. III, 1760 Procl. Rl. Poor, holed. Carrera. 1861 Rl. C.S. R within dotted circle. Good, v. rare. 1889 $\frac{1}{4}$ Rl. Unc. 3
793 Honduras. 1884, 50c. Costa Rica. 1864, 25c. '80, 50c. Good. 3
794 Haiti. 1883, 50c. Fine. San Domingo. 1891, 50c. and 1 Fc. Unc. 3

795 Tortola. TORTOLA in crude letters C.S. on ¼ of Mo. 4 Rl pc. Good, rare.   1

796 Ecuador. 1834, 2 Rls. U. S. Col. 1883, 50c. Lima. (16)71 Rl; 1718, 2 Rl (the last 2 cob); 1753, Rl; 1827, Llama ¼ Rl. Fair to fine.   6

797 Peru. 1826, ½ Rl; '27, 1 do.; also Dinero, ⅕ Sol and Peseta of later coinage. Good to fine.   5

798 Potosi. 1760, 4 Rls; '67, 2 do., cob. Fair. Bolivia. 1830, ½ (unc., a gem), 2 and 4 Rls, with bust of Bolivar. Fine.   5

799 Bolivia. 1864, ⅕ Bol. Arms. '65 Rl size. Beehive. Also 4 Rl size, busts of Melgarejo and M. Good to fine.   3

800 Chile. Ferd. VII, 1811, 2 Rls. Santiago mint. Mil. bust. 1855–61. ½, 1 Dcms and 20c. Condor flying. Gd to fine.   4

801 Venezuela. 1822, ¼ Rl. 19 within radiation. 1858, ½, 1 Rl. Lib. hd. 1874–86. ¼, 1, 2½ Bol., with Bolivar hd. V. gd.   6

802 British Guiana. Geo. III, 1816, ¼, 1 Guilder. V. gd, scarce.   2

803 Brazil. 1695, 320 Reis. 1784, 640 do. 1853, 500 do. Good to fine.   3

804 La Plata. 1815, 2, 4 Slds., Potosi mint. 1826, 2 do., Rioja mint. Cordova, 1855, ½ Rl. Uruguay, 1877, 10c. Good to fine.   5

805 England. Chas. I Shil. Fair. Chas. II, 1673 ½ Crown. Wm. and Mary, 3, 4d. Maundy. Anne, 1711 Shil. Good to fine.   5

806 Geo. III, 1808 Irish Bank Token. ½ Cwn. 1817, ½ Cwn. Both fair. '20, 6d., fine. Geo. IV, 1828 Lion Shil., good.   4

807 Wm. IV, 1834, 1½, 3d. Vic., 1838, 2, 3, 4d. '39, 1½d. Good to v. fine.   6

808 1848, 2d.; '54, 4d.; '61, Shil.; '66, 6d.; '72, 3d. Mostly fine.   5

809 1849 Godless Florin. Fine, scarce.   1

810 1887, 3d.; '88, 3, 6d.; '89, 3d. All Jubilee type. V. fine.   4

811 1893, 3, 6d. Shil., Florin, and ¼ Cwn. The new coinage. Unc.   5

812 Spain. Khalifs. Rahman III, 912-61; Hakam II, 961-76; Mohammed Ibn Edris, 1046-54; and two others, unattributed. Dirhems. Good to fine.   5

813 Phil. II, 4 Rls, fair. Phil. V, 1718, ½ do., good. Jos. Nap., 1813, 4 do., fair.   3

814 Ferd. VII, 1821, 10 Rls; size 33. Is. II, 1853, 10 do. S. 29. Good and fine.   2

815	Sweden. Adol. Fred., 1770, 1, 2 Dalers. V. good. 29–35.	2
816	Gust. Adol. IV, 1809 ; Chas. XIV, 1819, ⅙ Rixd. V. fine. 26.	2
817	Os. II, 10, 25, 50 Ore ; 1, 2 Kronor. 1883–90. Unc., brill.	5
818	Denmark. 1854 Rgdsdlr ; Geldern, 1738 Guld. Flanders. 1788–9, ¼, ½ Ecu. Good. 29 to 34.	4
819	Netherlands. 1843 Guld. Belgium. 1867, 1, 2 Fcs. Good to fine.	3
820	Bremen. 1840, 36 Gte. Hamburg. 1877, 2 Mks. Good.	2
821	Bruns.-Lun. Ernst Aug., 1693, ⅔ Thlr. Saxony. 1854, ⅙ do. Good.	2
822	Wurtemburg. Wm., 1841 Guld. German Emp. 1873 20 Pfg ; '76, 50 do. V. good.	3
823	Austria. Fran. Jos., 1859 Florin. Switzerland. 1851, ½ Fc ; '61, 1 do. ; '81, ½ do. Good to fine.	4
824	Italy. Nap., 1810, 10 Soldi ; Vic. Eman., 1862, 50c. ; '63, 1, 2 Fcs. Fair to fine.	4
825	Papal. Pius VI, 1796 Test. Fair. Greg. XIV, 1841, 5 Bai. ; Pius IX, 10, 20 Bai. and Lira, 1850–66. Good to unc.	5
826	Sardinia. 1815, 10 Grani. Unc. '28, 50c. Greece. 1873 Dchm. Roumania. 1873 Leu. Fair to good.	4
827	Russia. 1802, 10 Kop. Rare. 1853, 25 do. ; '64, 20 do. Fine and unc.	3
828	Turkey. 1293=1876, ¼, 1, 2, 5, 10 Piastres. 13 to 27. Fine to unc.	5
829	Duplicates of the 1, 2 and 5 Pias., with 2 smaller values earlier. Good to fine. 9 to 24.	5
830	Egypt. 1839–61. 10 Grusch. 28. Present coinage, 1 and 2 Piastres. 16, 19. Morocco. ½ and 1 Dirhem. 14, 17. Gd to unc.	5
831	Mombasa. British E. Africa. 2 Annas, ¼, ½, 1 Rupee, 1888–90. Unc.	4
832	German E. Africa. 1891, ¼, ½, 1 Rupee. Unc.	3
833	South African Rep. Paul Kruger, 1892, 3, 6d., 1, 2, 2½ Shil. Unc., about equal to proofs.	5
834	Eritrea. Umberto, 1890, 5 Ctmos, 1, 2 Lire. Unc.	3
835	Abyssinia. Menelik, 1894, 2, 4, 8 Guerche. King's bust r. ℞ Lion, Abyssinian date and legend. Unc. 19, 24, 30.	3
836	India. Moorshedabad Rupee. Vic., 1862, do. ; '80, " Empress " 2 Annas. Fine.	3

837 Madras. ¼ Pagoda. Hong Kong. Vic., 10, 20c. Good to
    fine.   3
838 Cambodia. Norodom, 1860, 50 Ctms, 2 Fçs. Unc.   2
839 Kwang-tung. Candareens and Mace. Sizes 15, 17, 23, 33.
    Unc.   4
840 Ind. Batavia. 1802, ¼, ½ Ship Guld. Straits. Vic., 10, 20c.
    Fine to unc.   4
841 Japan. Oblong Bu, 5, 10 Sen, present coinage. All fine.   3
842 Others, containing from 10c. to 20c. size, includes Bu. All
    different. Good to fine.   16
843 A selection of the duplicates of the preceding, 5 to 10c. size.
    All different. Good to fine.   17

CROWNS.

844 Mexico. 8 Rls, cob. ₽ | o—prob. Phil. III. Fair.   1
845 Ferd. VI, 1757, 8 Rls. Globes and pillar type. V. good.   1
846 Chas. III, 1766, 8 Rls. Type as last. About fine.   1
847 Chas. IV, 1807, 8 Rls. Bust type. V. fine.   1
848 Rep., 1863, 8 Rls. Lib. cap. V. fine. Empire, Max., 1866
    Peso. Fine.   2
849 Max., 1866 Peso. Rep., 1873, 8 Rls. Balance type. Good.   2
850 1872, 8 Rls. Balance type. Go. mint. '76, 8 do. Lib. cap.
    Fine.   2
851 1876, 8 Rls. Lib. cap. Fine. '90, 8 do., M. Unc.   2
852 1890, 8 Rls, Ga. mint. Unc., bril. '93, Ca. mint. Fine.   2
853 Guatemala. 1872 Peso. Justice std. Good.   1
854 Dominican Rep. 1891, 5 Fcs. Lib. hd l. Unc.   1
855 Colombia. Rep., 1836, 8 Rls. Fasces bet. cornucopias. Fine.   1
856 Ecuador. 1884 Sucre. Hd l. by *Heaton.* V. fine.   1
857 Peru. Chas. III, 1763, 8 Rls. Pillar type, Lima mint. Free
    Peru. 1822, 8 Rls. Good.   2
858 Lima. 1740, 8 Rls, cob money. Good for the coinage.   1
859 South Peru. 1837 Cuzco, 8 Rls. Mt., fort and sea. Very
    good. Bolivia. 1838, 8 Rls. Bolivar's bust. Fair.   2
860 Bolivia. 1838, 8 Rls. C. S. with face of sun on 5-ptd star,
    backed by arrow and quiver crossed. Good. Chile. 1877
    Peso. Fine.   2
861 Brazil. Peter I. 1695, 640 Reis. La Plata. 1834, 8 Slds.
    Sun in splendor. Good.   2

862	960 Reis. Cwnd arms C. S. on 8 Rls. Potosi mint, bust type, 1804. Fine. rare.	1
863	England. Chas. II, 1663 and '71 Cwns. Var. in bust. Fair.	2
864	Geo. III. 1804 Bk of Ireland, 6 Shil. Good, scarce.	1
865	Geo. IV. 1821 Cwn. ℟ St George and Dragon. Fair.	1
866	Victoria. 1893 Crown of the new coinage (succeeded Jubilee type). About unc.	1
867	France. Louis XV, 1774; do. XVI, 1781 Ecus. Good and v. fine.	2
868	Rep. An 7, Hercules type. Good. Nap. I, 1812, 5 Fcs. V. fair.	2
869	L. Phil., 1831 Fair. Rep. 1849 Hercules type. 5 Fcs.	2
870	Spain. Jos. Nap., 1812, 20 Rls. Fine.	1
871	Isabel II, 1854, 20 Rls. Fine.	1
872	Sweden. Adol. Fred., 1770, 3 Daler. S. M. Bust. Fine, rare. 40.	1
873	Denmark. Fred. III, 1659, 4 Mks. Arm from cloud, with sword, severs hand reaching for crown. Fine, initials scratched on *obv.* 41.	1
874	Fred. VII, 1848 Species, upon the death of Chris. VIII. Their hds upon opposite sides. Fine.	1
875	Flanders. 1755 M. Ther. Ecu. Cwnd arms. ℟ Brabant cross. Good.	1
876	1775 Sim. to last. Francis I, 1797 Bust. Ecus. Good.	2
877	1807 Ecu, var. of last. Fair. Belgium. Leop. II, 1869, 5 Fcs. Good.	2
878	Prussia. Fred., 1765 Thlr. eagle on trophy; 1767 Thlr. ℟ Arms in cwnd shld. Good.	2
879	1786 Trophy type. Fair. Fred. Wm., 1795. ℟ Arms suptd. Good. Thlrs.	2
880	Fred. Wm. III, 1815 Hd *r.*; 1818 Mil. bust *l.*; Wm., 1863 Thlrs. ·Good.	3
881	Hungary. Fred. I, 1555 Krem. Thlr. Bust. ℟ Arms K-B. Madonna. Fine.	1
882	Bavaria. Max. Jos., 1755 ℟ Patron Saint. Max. Jos. (King), 1813. ℟ Sword and sceptre. Thlrs. Good.	2
883	Louis I, 1837 Dbl. Thlr. Monetary union of So. German States. Fine, some slight scratches.	1
884	Bruns.-Lunbg. Geo., 1640 Wildman Thlr. Good.	1

885 Saxony. Ernest line, Fred. III, John and Geo., 1500–25 Thlr. Bust of Fred. ℞ Busts of John and George. About fine.

886 John Ernest and his seven bros., 1611 Thlr. 4 busts on either side. Fair.

887 Albert line, John, Geo. and Aug., 1597 ; Fred. Aug., 1841. Thlrs. Fair.

888 Henneburg. 1694 Thlr. PINGUESCIT DUM etc. A hen *r*. ℞ Saxon and Henneburg arms. Fine, scarce. 45.

889 Frankfort a/m 1862 Thlr. in remembrance of July shooting fest. Fine, *rev*. edge dent.

890 Zurich. 1753 Thlr. Lion *l*. sup. city arms. ℞ View of city. Fine.

891 Italy. Nap. I, 1808. V. fair. Vic. Em., 1874. Fine. 5 Fcs.

892 Lucca. 1748 Scudo. St. Martin and beggar. Nearly fine.

893 Tuscany. Cosmus III, 1677 Piastre. Bust *r*. ℞ John baptising. Good.

894 Sicily. Murat, 1813, 5 Lire. With his head. Good.

895 Russia. Peter the Gt, 1723 Rouble. Bust *r*. ℞ 4 Russian Ps in cross form. Fine.

896 Cath. II, 1762 Rouble. Bust *r*. Good. Alex. III, 1883 Coronation Rouble. ℞ Crown and sceptre. Nearly fine.

897 Turkey. Abdul Medjid, 20 Piastres, 1255, 7th year = 1845. Unc.

898 Abdul Hamid II, 20 Piastres, 1293, 2d year = 1878. V. fine.

899 Sierra Leone. 1791 Dollar. Prowling lion. ℞ The hand of a white and black man clasped. Good.

900 Eritrea. Umberto, 1891 Tallero or 5 Lire. Bust, large hd *r*. Unc., brill., a few light nicks.

901 Abyssinia. Menelik, 1894, 16 Guerche. Bust *r*. ℞ Lion. Unc., brill.

902 Madras. ½ Pagoda. God Swami. ℞ Pagoda, English value. Fine. 35½.

903 Siam. 2 Ticals, struck at Bangkok, 1868. Elephant *l*. ℞ 3 Pagodas. Ex. fine. 37.

904 Kwang-tung. 7 Mace 2 Candareens. Dragon. Unc. 39.

905 Japan. Yen, value in English. Fine.

906 Yen, value in Japanese. Nearly fine.

GOLD COINS.

907 **California.** 1852 Half Dol. D. N. beneath hd. V. fine.   1
908   1852 U. S. Assay office, 10 Dols. Eagle holds shield. ℞ 4
       line ins. V. good, a few nicks and edge dents.   1
909   1853 Half Dol., same type as 907. Unc.   1
910   1853 Half Dol., sim. to last, sq. top to 3. V. fine.   1
911   1854 Half Dol. Fine. 1860 Dol. Unc., both octagonal.   2
912   1870, '71 both oct., '71 date on *obv.* Half Dols. V. fine. 3
913   1874 Dol. '76 Quar. Dol. Both oct. and unc. '81 Half
       Dol. Good.   3
914   1881–86. Various Charms, size of Quar. and Half Dols. 3
       oct. Unc.   6
915   Rutherford, N. C. C. Bechtler Dol. Fine, 2 edge cuts.   1
916   **United States.** 1796 Eagle (10 Dols.). V. good, scarce. 1
917   1798 Half Eagle. Large eagle *rev.* V. fine.   1
918   1799 Eagle. Very fair.   1
919   1834 Quarter Eagle. New type, fine.   1
920   1853 Dollar. O. mint. V. fine.   1
921   1854 Dollar. V. fine.   1
922   1856 Dollar. V. good, some light scratches.   1
923   1856 Dollars. About as last.   2
924   1857 Dollar. V. fine.   1
925   1862 Dollar. V. fine.   1
926   1873 Dollar. V. fine.   1
927   1873 Dollar. Fine, light scratches. '74 do. Fine, *obv.* edge
       dent.   2
928   1874 Dollar. Fine, faint scratch.   1
929   1887 Dollar. V. fine.   1
930   1893 2½ Dols. Fine, light nicks.   1
931   **Foreign.** Mexico, 1886 ; Columbia, 1825. Pesos. Fine.   2
932   U. S. Colombia, 1873 ; New Granada, 1840 ; Chile, 1860.
       Pesos. Fine.   3
933   England. Geo. III, 1787 Spade Guinea and its half. Poor,
       loops removed.   2
934   1798 Hd by *Pingo.* Good. 1810 Hd by *Marchant.* Fine.
       ⅓ Guineas.   2
935   1820 Sovereign. Hd by *Pistrucci.* Fine, light scratches on
       obv.   1

48   AMERICAN MEDALS.

936 1892 Victoria, Sovereign. Fine.   1
937 France. Nap. III, 1855, 10 Francs. Good.   1
938 1866, 20 Francs. Laur. head. Nearly fine.   1
939 Spain. Ferd. VI, 1755 Seville mint. Good. 1757 Madrid
     mint. Fine. Escudos or ⅛ Doub.   2
940 Chas. III, 1760 and '83 Escudos. Two types, nearly fine.   2
941 1788 Escudo. Var. of last. Good. Portugal. John V, 400
     Reis. Fine. Abt Dol. size.   2
942 Germany. Wm., 1888, 10 Marks. Abt unc., brill.   1
943 Venice. Aloy. Macenigo II, 1700–07 Ducat. Nearly fine.   1
944 Turkey. 1223=1808 Piastre. Unc. 13. 1277=1861, 10
     Grusch. Nearly fine. 14. Japanese Yen (size of U. S.
     Dol.) Fine.   3

                        AMERICAN MEDALS.

945 **White Metal.** Washington, Witherspoon, Stonewall Jack-
     son, Columbus (by *Massonnet*), another with miniature
     ticket on *rev.* under mica, etc. Two in aluminum. Perfect.
     51 to 53.   8
946 Centennials, Conventions, Anc. and Hon. Artillery, Boston,
     National Drill, Wash., N. Y. World, etc. 1 scratched, other-
     wise all abt perfect. 43 to 51.   9
947 Centennials, Bi-Centennials, etc. Albany, Allegheny Co.,
     Georgia, Germantown, McConnellsburg, Portland, etc.
     Mostly perfect, 3 holed, as issued. 27 to 37.   16
948 Conventions, Expositions, etc. Atlanta, Buffalo, Chicago,
     Louisville, Phila., Pittsburgh ('79 and '91), Richmond, G.
     A. R., Robt Fulton, etc. Mostly perfect, 4 holed, as issued.
     22 to 40.   24
949 Benj. F. Butler. Oval placque. Bronzed. Perfect, 4¾ x 5¾
     inches.   1
950 **Brass.** Buckalew, Columbus (2, one by *Massonnet*, Æ gilt),
     Douglas, Fremont, Franklin, Fulton, Garfield (silvered).
     Perfect, 2 holed, as issued. 10, 19, 25, to 50.   8
951 Grant (2), Harrison (W. H.), Lincoln, McClellan, Penn, Wash-
     ington (2). Perfect, 20½ to 38.   8
952 Govt. Bldg, Chicago, Sage's Hist. Series (4), Vassar, Napo-
     leon Tea, 1895, etc. Perfect. 13 to 37.   13

954 Phila. Centl Commission Medal. Slightest blemishes. Æ
gilt. 57.   1

955 **Bronze.** Cass, Grant (2), Ericsson, Harrison (2), Hosack,
Lincoln, McClellan (2), Washington (3). Perfect, a few are
proofs. 18 to 38.   13

956 Baltimore, Md. Exp. 1889, New Haven Soldiers' Monument,
1887, Penn. Vols. All 37½. Springfield Antiquarians, Gt.
Eastern. Perfect.   5

957 Mass. 1888, Anc. and Hon. Arty. 44. Phila. 1876, Art Gal-
lery. 51. Cyrus W. Field, by *Lovett.* 51. Perfect.   3

958 Columbian Exp. 1892. Lib. head *l.* ℞ Columbus landing.
Another, by *Massonnet.* ℞ Bird's-eye view of Exp. Per-
fect. 50.   2

959 Danish Columbian, Columbus in stern of vessel. Perfect. 64.
Am. Inst. 1863, awarded to S. J. Pardessus. V. fine. 60.   2

960 Maj. Genl Gaines, Battle of Erie, 1814. Perfect. 65.   1

961 Maj. Genl Harrison, Battle of the Thames, 1813. Slight chaf-
ing on head, otherwise perfect. 65.   1

962 Maj. Genl And. Jackson, Battle of New Orleans, 1815. Perfect. 65.   1

963 Pres. And. Jackson, 1829. ℞ Pipe and tomahawk crossed,
etc. Perfect. 62.   1

964 Pres. Jas. K. Polk, 1845, Peace Medal, as last. Perfect. 62.   1

965 Gov. Isaac Shelby, Battle of the Thames, 1813. Perfect. 65.   1

966 Capt. Chas. Stewart, Capture of British warships, *Cyane* and
Levant, 1815. Perfect. 65.   1

967 Artist, Gilbert Stuart, by *Wright,* 1849, Am. Art Union. Fine. 64.   1

968 Maj. Genl Zac. Taylor, by *Wright,* Battle of Buena Vista, 1847.
V. fine. 90.   1

969 **Silver.** 1780 Escape of the Dutch fleet ; vessel *r.* *Ex.* IACOB
VAN DER | WINT. Betts 574. Fine. 31.   1

970 1781 Battle of Doggersbank. HOEZEE! DE BRIT, etc., vessels
in action. Betts 588. Fine. 30.   1

971 John Ericsson, by *Ahlborn.* ℞ The monitor he constructed
which spread consternation in Hampton Roads, Mch 9th,
1862. Perfect. 31.   1

972 **Politicals.** Scott, by *G. F. Thomas.* Balto. Conv. 1852.
" Queenstown," Canada, among his victories, named on *rev.*
Perfect, red copper, uncommon. 33½.   1

973　Others of Fillmore, Fremont (large), Douglas, Bell, Lincoln
(1860 and '64), McClellan, Grant, Seymour, Greeley, Tilden,
Garfield, Cleveland (1884 and '88), Blaine, and Harrison
(1888). A very choice collection, not often equalled within
the period, for rarity and preservation. W.m., brass and
copper. 6 holed as issued.　　　　　　　　　　　　44

FOREIGN MEDALS.

974　**White Metal.** Canada. P. of W., 1860 ; England, France,
Cologne, Chas. III's entry to Madrid, 1710 ; Jos. Corona-
nation, 1696 ; Chas. VI, 1717 and '31 (Peace of Vienna) ;
Russia, Cath. II, 1782 ; Turkey, Abdul-Medjid, 1854. Fine
to perfect, 24 to 64. Mostly of the larger size.　　　　14

975　**Bronze.** Venezuela, 1883. CENTENARIO DEL NATALICIO DE
BOLIVAR. Busts of Bolivar and Blanco conjoined. ℞ Tablet, inscribed. Slightly injured in centre of *rev.*, otherwise
fine. Very rare. 45.　　　　　　　　　　　　1

976　Holland. 1765 Medal relating to commerce. 44. 1807 The
Rhine Conduits. 47. Louvain City Hall, 1848. 50. Fine.　3

977　France. Marshal Saxe. Bust *r.* by *Dassier*. Defeat of Duke
of Cumberland at Laffeldt, 1747. Fine. A few nicks. 54.　1

978　Louis XV. Bust *l.* by *Caque*. 52. Louis Anton, Duke of
Angouleme. Bust *l.* by *Gayrard*. 40. Both fine.　　　2

979　Louis XV, Nap. I and III and Eugenie, also Exposition 1889.
(Brass.) 25 to 41. Fine to perfect.　　　　　　　　4

980　Louis XVIII and Chas. X, 1825. Hds conjoined *l.* Comple-
tion of the Paris Bourse. About perfect. 68.　　　　1

981　Napoleon III, 1852. Chronology of the Kings of France.
Small medallion of the Emperor in centre. Fine. 56½.　1

982　Expositions. 1855 (iron), 1878, with *Oudine's* hd of Concordia. V. fine. 50.　　　　　　　　　　　　　　2

983　Portugal. Exterior and interior views of the Cathedral of Ste.
Marie Belem at Lisbon, by *Weiner*. About perfect. 60.　1

984　Germany. 1889 Wm. III. Visit to England. Bust *l.* by
Lauer. ℞ Naval review. Fine. 59.　　　　　　　1

985　The Port of Kiel, 1847. 50. Rendsburg fortress, 1848. 42.
Witten Poultry Show. 40. War Medal, 1870-71, "For
faithfulness to duty in war." Iron, with loop and ring. 28.
Fine to perfect.　　　　　　　　　　　　　　4

986 Geneva. 1738 Concordia Geneva Restituta, by *Dassier.* 55.
1806 Genuense Ptochotrophium. Almshouse Medal of
Merit. 41. Fine. 2

987 Sardinia. Vic. Eman. 1814 Visit to Turin. Bust *r.* 52.
Hermolaus III of Pisa. Bust *r.* Market of Verona re-
stored. 54. Fine. 2

988 Cluysenaar, Belgian architect. Bust *l.* by *Hart.* ℞ Interior
view of hall of the Royal Society of Grand Harmony. V.
fine. 68. 1

989 Louis Marie de Cormenin, French magistrate and political
writer; Zanotti, Italian astronomer, etc. Poor to fine. 40
to 67. 6

990 Guttenburg, inventor of printing. 25. Rubens, painter. 45.
Perfect. 2

991 Lt.-Gen. Lord Lynedock, by *Webb.* ℞ St. Sebastian, 1813,
by *Mills.* Fine. 41. 1

992 Montesquieu, Chas. De S., French jurist, philosopher, etc.,
1755, by *Dassier.* Fine. 60. 1

993 Rembrandt. Bust *l.* by *De Vries*, 1873. ℞ Scene from his
celebrated painting, "La Ronde de Nuit." One of the
largest medals ever struck from dies. About perfect. 109. 1

994 **Silver.** Guanabacoa. Is. II, 1834 Procl. Medal. Spanish
arms. ℞ City arms. Good, holed. 24. Lima, 1868 Sun
in splendor. ℞ Bajo la, etc., in 8 lines. V. fine. 24. Also
Medalet of the Vic. Jubilee in U. S. 16. 3

995 France. Oct. Jetons by Societies of Commerce, time of Nap.
I. 30 and 34. Peace of Ryswick, 1697. 20. Fine. 3

AN IOWA CONSIGNMENT.

996 **Colonial.** Mass., 1652 Pine Tree Sixpence. Good, with
rev. not well centred. 1

997 1787 Half Cent and Cent. V. fair. 2

998 Washington, 1783 Unity Cent, also dbl hd Cent. Good. 2

999 1791 The large eagle Cent. Rather poor, rare. 1

1000 1792 Half Disme. Good, rare. 1

1001 **U. S. Silver.** Trimes. 1851 O. mint. Unc. '54 Fine.
'55 Fair. '57 Unc. 4

1002 1863 Proof, slight tarnish. 1

1003 1866 Brilliant proof. 1

1004   1870 Brilliant proof.
1005   1872 V. fine. '73 Proof, slight tarnish.
1006   Half Dimes. 1795 Nearly fine.
1007   1795 Fair. 1829 Unc., brill.
1008   1800 LIBEKTY. Extra fine, small nick on neck.
1009   Five Cents, Nickel. 1867 Stars and bars. Proof, v. rare.
1010   1877 Proof, rare.
1011   Dimes. 1796 Fine, a few slight nicks.
1012   1798 Perfect date. Stars *l*. worn smooth, otherwise v. fair.
1013   1800 Very good.
1014   Twenty Cents. 1877 Proof, somewhat impaired.
1015   Quar. Dols. 1796 Good, rare.
1016   1804 Good, oftener found poor.
1017   1825 over '23 and '22. V. good.
1018   1825 over '24. Fine.
1019   1853 Without arrows. Good, rare.
1020   1893 Isabel Columbian. Unc., brill.
1021   1893 Others, quite as last.
1022   1893 Others, the same.
1023   Half Dols. 1794 V. good, a few light dents and scratches on *obv.* Rare.
1024   1795 Very good.
1025   1801 Very good, rare.
1026   1803 Nearly fine.
1027   1803, '05 (2). Good.
1028   1805 Nearly fine.
1029   1836 Milled edge. Fine, scarce.
1030   Dollars. 1795 Head. Nearly fine, two nicks on *obv.*
1031   1797, 6 stars facing. Very good.
1032   1797 Another from same dies as last, and about as good.
1033   1800 Fine. Stars all sharp.
1034   1801 Good.
1035   1802 Perfect date. V. fine. Short scratch below y in Liberty, and small dent near first star *l*.
1036   1836 Gobrecht on base. Proof. Very slightly haymarked.
1037   1841 Very fine.
1038   1878 Standard. 8 feathers in eagle's tail. Unc., brill., nick on cheek.
1039   1879 Trade. Proof.

1040 **U. S. Gold.** Quar. Dols. 1869 Octagonal. Unc., edge
test cut. 1
1041 1870 Unc. 1
1042 1873 Unc. 1
1043 Half Dollars, 1864. Octagonal. Unc. 1
1044 1870 Unc., equal to proof. 1
1045 Dollars. 1849 O. mint. Good. 1
1046 1850 Fine. 1
1047 1851 Very fine. 1
1048 1852 Unc., a few light nicks. 1
1049 1852 Very fine. 1
1050 1853 Very fine. 1
1051 1854 Uncirculated. 1
1052 1862 Uncirculated. 1
1053 1870 Uncirculated. 1
1054 1871 Fine. 1
1055 1873 California octagonal. V. fine, bril., rare. 1
1056 1873 A few slight scratches, otherwise unc. 1
1057 1876 Proof, scratch on *obv.* field. 1
1058 1878 Uncirculated. 1
1059 1879 Uncirculated. 1
1060 1881 Uncirculated. 1
1061 1883 Uncirculated. 1
1062 1885 Proof, faint scratch on face. 1
1063 1887 Uncirculated. 1
1064 1888 Uncirculated. 1
1065 1889 Uncirculated. 1
1066 Two and a-half Dollars. 1836 Very fine. 1
1067 Three Dollars. 1854 V. fine, slightest marks of wear. 1
1068 1863 Very good, light nicks. 1
1069 1878 Proof. 1
1070 1878 Fine, brill. 1
1071 1878 Unc., a few light nicks. 1
1072 1882 Very fine. 1
1073 1882 Proof, scarce. 1
1074 1883 Unc., a few light nicks, rare. 1
1075 1888 Condition as last. 1
1076 Half Eagle (Five Dollars), 1799. V. fine, shows but trifling
wear. 1

1077 1803 over '02. Very fine.   1
1078 **U. S. Fractional Currency.** (New and crisp, unless
      otherwise stated.) 1st issue, 5, 10, 25, 50c., without A B CO
      on *rev.* Perforated edges. 10c. perfect, others v. fine.
      The 50c. has perforation at bottom only.   4
1079 A set as last, fronts and backs separate, wide margins.   4
1080 5, 10, 25, 50c., with A B CO. Plain edges. A few unimpor-
      tant defects.   4
1081 2nd issue. Washington in bronze oval. 5, 10, 25, 50c. The
      last two fibre paper.   4
1082 A set as last, fronts and backs separate. Plain paper,
      trimmed margins.   4
1083 As last. Separate backs of 5, 10 (with gilt oval on *rev.*),
      25c., and *obv.* of 50c. (2, light and heavy paper). All on
      fibre paper, each with two cancellations, and " SPECIMEN "
      stamped on face. V. rare. It is doubtful if they can be
      duplicated.   5
1084 3d issue, 3c. Bust of Wash. Light and dark curtain.   2
1085 3c. Light curtain. 5c. Clark, 10c. Wash., 25c. Fessenden.   4
1086 5c. Clark, 10c. Wash., 25c. Fessenden.   3
1087 25c. Fessenden. Heavy fibre paper. Rare.   1
1088 25c. Fessenden, as last ; slight traces of fold through centre.   1
1089 25c. Fessenden. Fronts only, without 25 in gilt at sides.
      Plain and fibre paper ; 5 cancellations and " SPECIMEN " on
      each. V. rare.   2
1090 50c. Justice. Heavy fibre paper ; slight traces of fold in
      centre.   1
1091 50c. Spinner.   1
1092 3c. Dark curtain, 10c. Wash., 25c. Fess., 50c. Spinner. Fronts
      and backs separate, and wide margins, except 25c.   4
1093 Red backs. 5c. Clark.   1
1094 5c. Clark, 10c. Wash. (with auto. sig.). Separate backs and
      fronts, wide margins.   2
1095 5c. Clark, 10c. Wash., 25c. Fess., 50c. Justice (auto. and litho.
      sigs.), 50c. Spinner. Fronts and backs separate, margins
      trimmed.   6
1096 4th Issue. 10c. Liberty, 15c. Columbia, 25c. Wash. Pink
      silk fibre paper.   3
1097 10c. Lib., 15c. Col., 25c. Wash. Blue, red ends, violet fibre.   3

1098 10c. Lib., fibre paper; 15c. Col., plain paper; 50c. Stanton.   3
1099 5th Issue. 10c. Meredith, green seal; 50c. Dexter.   2
1100 50c. Crawford, 25c. Walker, with long key.   2
1101 10c. Meredith, 25c. Walker, 50c. Crawford. All with short
    key.   3
1102 10c. Meredith, 25c. Walker (2), short keys.   3
1103 15c. Grant and Sherman, red back, auto. sig. of Allison and
    Spinner. Separate back and front, wide margins, pin-holes
    on one end of back; very rare.   1
1104 15c. as last. Autos. of Jeffries and Spinner. Green back,
    margins cut but not to frame line; v. rare.   1
1105 15c. precisely as last. Margins cut close.   1
1106 15c. as last, with lith. sigs. Margins trimmed close.   1
1107 15c. precisely as last. Fine.   1
1108 Various. 5c. (5, four of 1st issue), 15c., 50c. from circulation.
    Some very good; also unmatched separate fronts and backs
    (red and green), with autos. of Colby and Spinner on 50c.;
    all clean.   15

A MARYLAND CONSIGNMENT.

1109 Half Cents, 1794. V. good.   1
1110 1794 Var. of last. '95 Lettered edge. Good.   2
1111 1797, 1800, '03, '04 (2 var.), '05, '06 (2 var.), '07, '08. Poor
    to good. The better prevail.   10
1112 1802 Poor, rare.   1
1113 1809, '10, good; '11, v. fair.   3
1114 1811 (2), '25 (2), '26, '28 (3, one with 12s). V. fair to v.
    good.   8
1115 1829, '32 to '35, '49, '50, '51, '53 to '57. Good to v. fine.   13
1116 Cents. 1793 Wreath, vine and bars. V. fair.   1
1117 1794 Hays 33, 45 (2). Fair and good.   3
1118 1795 Plain edge (2). Lettered do. '97, '98 (2 var.), 1800
    (2 var.) Poor to good.   8
1119 1796 Lib. cap. V. good, scratch on head.   1
1120 1796 LIHERTY. V. fair, rare.   1
1121 1801 (2 var.), '02, '03 (2 var.), '05 (2 var.), '06. Mostly good.   8
1122 1803 (2 var.), '05, '06, '07 (2 var.), '08, '10. Fair and good.   8
1123 1806 Nearly fine; dark green patination.   1
1124 1806 Very good.   1

1125 1806 V. good, but corroded. '08 Nearly fine. Med. light
      olive.   2
1126 1810 Fine. '11 Perfect date, fair.   2
1127 1811 Perfect date, good.   1
1128 1812, '13, '14, plain 4. V. good.   3
1129 1812, '13 (2), '14 (2 var.), '16, '17, (13 and 15 stars.) Fair to
      good. Most of latter.   8
1130 1814, '17 (13s., 2 var., also 15s.), '18 (unc., some nicks), '19,
      sm. and lge date. Both fine ; others fair and good.   7
1131 1819 over '18, and perfect date, '20 to '23. Fair and good.
      Most of latter.   6
1132 1820 Unc., red.   1
1133 1821 Poor. '23 Good, but dark with corrosion. '24 Good.
      '25 V. good.   4
1134 1823 over '22. Good.   1
1135 1824, '25, '26. Nearly fine.   3
1136 1826, '27, '28 sm. date, '29, '30, '31. Mostly good.   6
1137 1827, '28 sm. and lge date, '29, '30. V. good, nearly fine.   5
1138 1828 Sm. date, '32 sm. and large letters, '33 (2), '34 (2), '35.
      Good.   8
1139 1833 Very fine, a few light nicks, medium olive.   1
1140 1834, '35 new head. Both fine.   2
1141 1834, '35 old head, '36. V. good, 2 nearly fine.   3
1142 1836 Good. '37 Plain hair cord. Very fine. Also beaded,
      good. '38 V. fine.   4
1143 1837 Plain hair cord. V. fine and sharp, slightest marks of
      circulation.   1
1144 1837 Plain hair cord (2), 38 (2). Good to fine.   4
1145 1838 Slight nicks on *obv.*, no other indications of wear, med.
      olive.   1
1146 1839 over '36. Nearly good, rare.   1
1147 1839 Hd of '38, Silly and Booby, and hd of '40. V. good to
      nearly fine.   4
1148 1839 Booby, '40 Sm. and large date, '42 Sm. and large date.
      Good and v. good.   5
1149 1840 Sm. date, '43, Hd of '42, '44, 45. Good to fine.   4
1150 1840 Large date. Unc., a few light nicks, med. light olive.   1
1151 1841 Condition as last.   1
1152 1845 (2), '46, '48, '49 (2), '50, '54. Mostly fine.   8

1153 1850 Unc., red. 1
1154 1851, '53. Unc., red. '54 Same condition, but not so bright. 3
1155 1855, '56, both with straight and italic 5s, '57 large date (2).
V. good to fine. 6
1156 1857 Sm. date. V. good. Large date. Fine. 2
1157 1856 Flying eagle, nickel. V. good, rare. 1
1158 Hard Times Tokens. Boar running ; Jackson with purse
and sword ; large-bellied donkey, etc. Low. 4, 8, 16, 18,
21, 22, 24, 25, 26 and 34. Good to fine. 10
1159 Hd with masculine features. ℞ "Not one cent." Holed.
Hd with short chin, no dash under cent. Fair. L. 35, 36.
Both rare. 2
1160 Others. L. 38 to 45, 49, 51 to 54 ; the last " Half cent worth
of pure copper." Fair to fine, mostly good. 13
1161 Others. L. 60, 62, 63, 65, 66, 69, 74, 78, 79, 80. One poor,
others good to fine. 19
1162 Bust of Van Buren. ℞ The Independant (sic) Sub-Treasury.
Brass. 82. Holed, as all are. V. good, rare. 1
1163 Others. L. 84, 85, 86, 88, 90, 92, 93, 94. Good to fine. 8
1164 Duplicates of Hard Times Tokens, 19 (13 var.), with two
Washington Unity Cents, 1783. Mostly good, some fine. 21
1165 1783 Wash. Unity Cent. Nearly fine ; not often equalled. 1

A MICHIGAN CONSIGNMENT.

1166 Half Cents. 1793 Very fair. 1
1167 1805, '06, '09, '25, '32, '56. Good to fine. 6
1168 Cents. 1809 V. fair, rare. 1
1169 1819, '36, '40, '48, '49. Two Cents. 1867, '68, '69, 71, '72.
Good to unc. 10
1170 Trimes, silver. 1851 O. mint, '58, '61, '62, '68 (proof), '70,
'71 (proof), '72. Fine to unc. 8
1171 Three Cents, nickel. 1867, '68, '69, '71, '72, '74, '75, '76,
'79, '80, '81, '82. Mostly unc. 12
1172 Half Dimes. 1829, '30, '31, '59. Fine to unc. 4
1173 Five Cents, nickel. 1867, '68, '69, '71, '72, '74, '75, '76, '79
to '82, '88, '89. Unc. and proof, 2 spotted. 14
1174 Dimes. 1807, 1 each, poor and good ; '39, sharp and brill. ;
'50, fine ; '62, '73, unc. ; '75, '76, proofs. 8

1175 1879, '80 to '82. Proofs. '88 Unc.
1176 1889 to '93. Proofs.
1177 Twenty Cents. 1875 A trifle circulated. '76 V. fine.
1178 Quar. Dols. 1805 Poor. '32 Nearly fine.
1179 1852 Nearly fine, scarce.
1180 1853 Arrows. Unc. '54 A little less than unc.
1181 1855, '56. Ext. fine. '62 Unc.
1182 1863 Proof.
1183 1864 Proof.
1184 1865, '66. Proofs.
1185 1876 Proof, slight blemishes. '78 Fine.
1186 Half Dols. 1808 Fair. '11 V. good.
1187 1820 Good, edge clipped. '24 Fair.
1188 1825, '36. Fair, the latter scratched.
1189 1859 About unc. '77 S. mint. V. fine.
1190 Dollars. 1796 Sm. date. About gd, light scratches on *obv*.
1191 1842 Nearly fine.
1192 1854 Very good, scarce.
1193 1880 Trade. Proof, brilliancy slightly impaired.
1194 1888 O. mint. Unc., nicks on head.
1195 Hard Times Tokens (all marked with Low's number in ink, on the piece). Boar *l.*, nose points to space between H and c. ℞ Jackson with broad shoulders. L. 6. Fine, scarce.
1196 Boar *l.*, nose points to c in Credit. *Rev.* from same die as last. L. 7. Brass. Black from passing through fire, otherwise good and very rare.
1197 Jackson with purse and sword. "Plain" weakly struck. L. 8. Unc., med. olive, a rare condition.
1198 Others. L. 8, 16, 21, 22, 24, 25, 34, 38, 39, 41. Mostly v. fine.
1199 Female hd *l.* 13 stars. Fine; even the "Not" remains unscratched. L. 27. Rare.
1200 Similar. Smaller hd, 15 stars, 2 of them small. L. 28. V. good. "Not" unscratched. Rare.
1201 United hd. L. 29. Answers same description as last in every respect.
1202 Female hd, ugly features. ℞ "Not one cent," etc. L. 34. Weak in centre of *rev.*, as invariably the case with this piece. Rare.

1203 Female hd; short chin, *without* dash below cent. L. 36.
      Fair. Rare.   1
1204 Others. L. 42, 44, 49, 50, 52, 53, 62, 64, 65, 66. Good to
      fine, the last partly bright.   10
1205 Steer stdg. " A friend to the constitution." L. 56. V. fair,
      cut on edge. Rare.   1
1206 Others. L. 67 to 70 (scarce), 74 (fair), 79, 80 (v. fine, light
      olive), 84, 85, 86. Good to fine.   10
1207 Three Cents. Arms of New York. Feuchtwanger's com-
      position. L. 75. Good.   1
1208 Others. L. 88, 89. Both v. fine and light olive ; the latter
      rare.   2
1209 Others. L. 92, 93, 94 ; also duplicates of 16, 22, 25, 34, 50,
      70. Fair to good.   9
1210 Copper Coins and Tokens. Mexico, 1895 ; English and Irish
      Tokens, Halfpennies, 7, Pennies, 6, one with a keystone.
      Very good ; also medal Chas. XV, Sweden. Poor to unc.   17
1211 Silver. Mexico. Chas. IV, 1796. Bust of the King and
      Queen. ℞ Equestrian statue. Fisher, 106. Good. 32.   1
1212 Church Medal, 1797. Los Remedios Statue. Oval, with
      loop. 28 x 34. Fis., 100. Good. Another in brass of a
      later period. Fine. 31.   2
1213 Ferd. VII, 1808 Procl. 2 Rls. V. gd. Another, for Oaxaca,
      with arms of the city. V. fine, but holed near edge. Fis.
      122, 481.   2
1214 Agustin, 1822, upon his inauguration. Eagle on cactus. Fis.
      188. Fine. 34.   1
1215 Rep. (1867), War Medal. Defending of the Rep. against
      France. Inscribed circular centre on cross intersected with
      rays. Loop. Fis. 283. Fine, rare. *Brass.* 46½.   1
1216 1877 Sociedad de Socorres, etc. Baker working at oven.
      Loop, ring and bar. Fis. 305. V. fine, rare. 31½.   1
1217 Masonic. o.·. DE GUADALAJARA 5631, in field on triangle
      LOG.·. | SOLOMON | N.·. 36 ℞ Dome with 3 pillars on circle
      of steps. Loop, ring and ribbon. V. fine. 35. Marvin 966.   1
1218 Half Rls of 1860, '62. Poor and fair. 30 Pence, Irish, 1808.
      Good.   3
1219 1892 8 Rls, Zac. mint. Unc., brilliant.   1
1220 1892 Another as last, but not quite its equal.   1

1221   Scotland. Mary I, 1557 Testoon. Arms, M–R. ℞ Cross, date on both sides. Good.   1

THE PROPERTY OF W. E. RICHEY.

1222   Copper Coins. Canada (3), U. S. Cents, 1827 to '57, consecutive from '42. Poor to good.   27

1223   W. I. Islands, So. Am., including Paraguay, Bocholt, X Heller, Russia (large), Viterbo, Gubbio, Sicily, with hd of Chas. V, India, Corea, etc. Good to fine.   40

1224   Sweden. Fred. I, 1726 Half Daler. Plate money. $3\frac{1}{2}$ x $3\frac{1}{2}$ inches. Fair.   1

1225   Ancient. Egypt. Ptol. VI, (size 41), Bactria, Eucratides (square), Byzantine; 8 reigns between A. D. 527 and 1203. All attributed, in separate envelopes, including 1 concave. Poor to good.   10

1226   White Metal Medals. American 8, Foreign 5. Includes the four Georges, peace of Rastadt, battle of Alma, etc. Fine to perfect, 1 holed; also Washington, "I cannot tell a lie," in wood.   14

1227   Small silver. U. S., 1830 Dime; '32 Half do. Mexico, Chas. and Joanna, 2 Rls. Guat., $\frac{1}{4}$ do. U. S. Col., 50c. Good to fine.   5

1228   England. Henry III, Penny; Henry VIII, Groat; Mary, Groat; Eliz., Shil. Fair to good.   4

1229   Chas. II, 1677, $\frac{1}{2}$ Cwn. Ireland. James I, 6d. France. Louis XV, 1751, $\frac{1}{4}$ Ecu. Spain. Ferd. and Is., Rl., nearly fine, others poor and fair.   4

1230   Sweden, 1710, 5 Ore. Denmark. 1644, 2 Marks, with Hebrew letters on *rev.*; 1875, Krone. Hamburg. Shil., 1727, etc. Good.   5

1231   Brandenburg. 1693, $\frac{3}{4}$ Thaler. Cleves. 1666, $\frac{1}{3}$ do. Saxony. 1614, $\frac{2}{3}$ do. All with bust. Good to fine.   3

1232   Saxony. 1694, $\frac{2}{3}$ Thlr. Hungary. 1710 and '90, $\frac{1}{2}$ do. Good to fine.   3

1233   Poland. 1548 and 1622, 3 Gros. Tuscany. 1675, Testone. John Baptist sitg. Papal. Sede Vacante, 1549–50 to Pius IX, small coins, Grosso size. Good to fine.   8

1234   Persia. 1 Kran of the present coinage. Lion *l.* Travancore. Deity std. Japan. 10 Sen. Good to fine.   3

1235 Dollar size. U. S. 1795 Dol. Head. Fine, a few light scratches. 1
1236 1878 Trade, S. mint. Good. Mexico. 1888 Ho. mint. Fine, brill. 2
1237 Mexico. Max., 1866 Peso. Fine. 1
1238 Bolivia. 1838 8 Slds. Holed, good. La Plata. 1815 8 Rls. Sun in splendor. Nearly fine. 2
1239 France. Nap. I, 1806 5 Fcs. Prussia. Fred. the Gt, 1786 Thlr. V. fair. 2
1240 Austria. M. Theresa, 1780 Levant Thlr. Fine. 1
1241 Russia. Peter the Gt, 1709 Medallic Rouble on victory over the Swedes at Pultowa. Loop removed. *Obv.* has a bad defect in planchet; rare. 1
1242 Peter the Gt, 1721 (in Russian) Rouble. Bust *r.* V. good. 1
1243 Cath. II, 1784 Rouble. Turkey. Large base coin, size 39. Good. 2
1244 Kwang-tung. 7 Mace 2 Candareens. Dragon. V. fine. 1
1245 Medals, etc. Sweden. Gust. Adolph., 1632 Mortuary Medal in silver. Bust facing. ℞ Sword in hand. Fine, *obv.* field burnished. 43. 1
1246 China. Temple Medal. Oval, 21 x 36, square hole within arched centre. Copper. 1
1247 Jetons. Holland. 1544 to '64. Fully attributed in separate envelopes, as are also the three following lots. Mostly fine. 7
1248 France. Hy II, 1557, to Louis XIV, 1693. Mostly good to fine. 14
1249 Others. Louis XIV, 1698, to Louis XV, with one of Nap. I, 1804. Condition as last. 14
1250 Artois. Louis XIV, 1, and others of Louis XV, with vars. of heads, several of which are from same dies as the Canadian Jetons, etc. Copper and brass. Mostly fine. 10
1251 Others. Louis XIV, XV and XVI, and Nap. I. Brass, mostly fine, with 5 in copper. Fair. 17
1252 Germany. The works of Laufer, 5 (1 in dup.), in copper, and Kranwinckel with his ship, brass. Fair to fine. 6